Coping with standards,
tests, and accountability

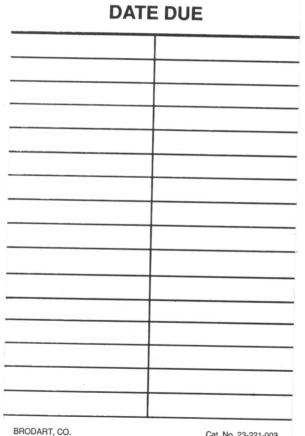

DATE DUE

Coping with
STANDARDS, TESTS,
and ACCOUNTABILITY:
Voices from the Classroom

Coping with
STANDARDS, TESTS,
and ACCOUNTABILITY:
Voices from the Classroom

By Allan A. Glatthorn and Jean Fontana

NEA Teaching and Learning Division

An NEA Professional Library Publication

Library of Congress Cataloging-in-Publication Data

Coping with standards, tests, and accountability: voices from the classroom/[edited] by
Allan A. Glatthorn and Jean Fontana.
        p. cm.
    Includes bibliographical references.
    ISBN 0-8106-2015-4 (alk. paper)
    1. Education—Standards—United States. 2. Educational tests and measurements—
United States. 3. Educational accountability—United States. I. Title: Standards, tests,
and accountability. II. Glatthorn, Allan A., 1924-III. Fontana, Jean.

LB3060.83.C66   2000
379.1'58—dc21

                                                        00-041584

DEDICATION

This book is dedicated to all those classroom teachers whose voices are seldom heard or heeded.

CONTENTS

PREFACE

Until now most of the published articles about curriculum standards, tests, and accountability have been written by policy makers, university professors, and school administrators. We hope that this book will correct that imbalance somewhat by finally letting current and recent teachers speak for themselves.

We intentionally did not select teachers who seemed to have a point of view that agreed with ours. Instead, we began by searching for those who already had published an article that gave evidence that they could write clearly and effectively. We began with the naive belief that teachers would be enthusiastic about the opportunity to speak to a nationwide audience. Instead, we found, to our dismay, that several of the teachers we approached turned us down. We then attempted to get a varied regional representation. Finally, we tried to have a group of teacher-authors who had varied teaching assignments. We believe that we were successful in identifying teachers who had something important to say about these crucial issues. We should note that some of those who were teachers when we first contacted them are now administrators or supervisors.

The first chapter by Glatthorn summarizes the research relating to how teachers make choices about content; the chapter is intended to present a general picture of the teacher as a decision maker who is rarely a slavish adherent of state directives. The next several chapters present the personal views of the classroom teacher-authors about standards, high-stakes tests, and accountability. The last two chapters by the editors provide a summary and a look ahead.

ACKNOWLEDGMENTS

First of all, we acknowledge our sincere gratitude to the classroom teachers who have contributed to this work. We know how busy all teachers are—and we express our thanks that these fine educators were willing to take the time from their busy schedules to write and revise. We also appreciate the continuing support provided by Timothy Crawford of the National Education Association, who encouraged us to publish this work and gave us considerable help in bringing the book to a publishable state. Finally, our families were both patient and encouraging. We especially learned first-hand that behind every successful author is a loving and patient spouse.

Allan Glatthorn and Jean Fontana

1

FROM POLICY TO PRACTICE:
THE RESEARCH
by Allan A. Glatthorn

The purpose of this introductory chapter is to review the research in order to provide a context for the personal statements in the chapters that follow. In general, the research suggests that state educational policies undergo several transformations before they are operationalized in classrooms. Figure 1.1 is a schematic showing how teachers interpret state policies and examine other factors in making classroom decisions.

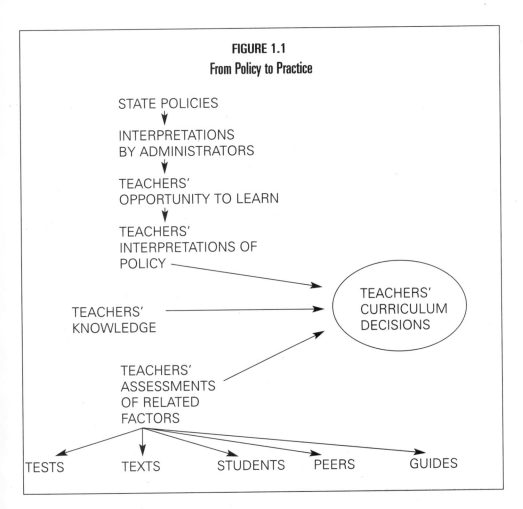

FIGURE 1.1
From Policy to Practice

STATE POLICIES

INTERPRETATIONS
BY ADMINISTRATORS

TEACHERS'
OPPORTUNITY TO LEARN

TEACHERS'
INTERPRETATIONS OF
POLICY

TEACHERS'
KNOWLEDGE

TEACHERS'
ASSESSMENTS
OF RELATED
FACTORS

TEACHERS'
CURRICULUM
DECISIONS

TESTS   TEXTS   STUDENTS   PEERS   GUIDES

The Complications of State Policies

The complications of implementing state policies begin in the halls of state legislatures where these policies are developed and adopted. As Darling-Hammond (1990) notes, legislators give much more attention to the development of policies than they do to the implementation of those policies. The policies they develop seem to suffer from three problems that affect implementation. First, they are often vague about specifics, so that educators are left to fill in the details. Administrators and teachers then fill in those details in a highly individualized manner. Also, the policies often contradict each other. Cohen and Ball (1990) note the inherent contradictions between policies designed to emphasize "the basics" and those that support critical thinking. Stressing the basics usually means using direct instruction and assigning drill and practice. On the other hand, developing critical thinking requires a problem-solving approach and reflective discussion. Noble and Smith (1994) point out that the new Arizona state testing program, which endorsed performance-based tests and a constructivist view of teaching and learning, was imposed in a manner that represented a behaviorist view of the change process.

Finally, legislators are just as susceptible to faddism as educators are. Thus, Pennsylvania lawmakers embraced Outcomes-Based Education until a storm of citizen protest caused them to jettison it. They then endorsed curriculum standards, confusing school administrators who had just finished developing outcomes-based curricula.

The Interpretations of Administrators

Those vague and conflicting policies are then transmitted through channels to district and school administrators who are already inundated with communications from the state, the regional service center, the school board, teachers, and parents. As they examine the new state policies, they bring to bear their own biases, prior knowledge, and agendas—all of which influence how they understand and communicate the information received from the state. Darling-Hammond (1990) points out that teachers thus receive messages from legislators through a filter, with much of the supporting information and contextual clues screened out by local administrators. For example, one principal might selectively emphasize the incentives in a new accountability program, while another principal in the same district might focus on the punitive aspects of the program.

Teachers' Limited Opportunities To Learn

The second place where distortion occurs is with teachers' opportunity to learn about new policies. As Cohen (1995) indicates, teachers seem to learn more about state policies from unofficial sources than they do from official ones. Typically, teachers read about policies in the educational press, learn about them in graduate courses, or hear them discussed at meetings of professional organizations. Teachers who are professionally active have one understanding of policies; those who are less professionally involved have a different and more limited understanding.

Teachers' Personal Practical Knowledge

A powerful factor in the way policies become transmuted is teachers' "personal practical knowledge," a term used by Elbaz (1983) and Clandinin (1986) to denote the special knowledge that each teacher brings to bear upon curriculum decision making. The teachers in Cornbleth's (1995) study reported that their own personal beliefs and priorities were the most important factors in deciding what to teach.

To understand personal practical knowledge, consider how the elements below would impact on a somewhat traditional teacher who is expected to emphasize critical thinking and problem solving.

- Images of self, the classroom, and the subject. ("Sometimes I feel these students are bumps on a log who can never learn to think critically.")

- Rules of thumb and craft knowledge. ("If it's Friday, give them easy seat work and don't try to do problem solving.")

- Knowledge of students, curriculum, the subjects, school, and community. ("Parents want these kids to learn grammar, not to think critically.")

- Personal beliefs and values. ("Critical thinking is OK, but it doesn't mean challenging the teacher.")

This personal practical knowledge obviously affects how teachers interpret policy, how they assess related factors, and how they make curriculum decisions.

Teachers' Interpretations of Policy

As might be expected from the preceding analyses, teachers' interpretations of the same policy vary significantly. And the evidence suggests, that since teachers have wide latitude, these varied interpretations proliferate. Sykes (1990) notes several organizational factors that seem to give teachers much discretion, thus operating against the uniform application of curriculum standards.

The technology of teaching and curriculum-making lacks sufficient detail. The ambiguity gives teachers some room for their own interpretations.

- Administrator oversight of teaching is weak or absent. Teachers know that they can close their doors and do what they wish.

- The preferences of clients (students and parents) seem to exert little influence. While teachers are sensitive to student moods, they usually are not concerned about student preferences for content.

- Professional norms (such as whether to make yearly plans) are remote or inconclusive. As noted below, teachers are sensitive to peer pressures, but the norms are not strong enough to effect standardization.

Given this set of conditions, teachers feel free to develop their own interpretations of policy, which in general represent a synthesis of the old and the new. As Cohen and Ball (1990) note, teachers integrate new policies into their existing practice. For this reason most teachers do not appear to be troubled by seeming contradictions in state policies.

Consider an English teacher strongly committed to using direct instruction to teach students the formula of the "500-word theme," complete with thesis statement, five paragraphs, and topic sentences. The state develops a curriculum framework emphasizing the writing process; the district follows up with a "talk-at-you" workshop explaining how to teach the writing process. The traditional teacher attends, interprets what she or he hears, and returns to the classroom, using direct instruction to teach the writing process as it applies to the 500-word theme. All that seems to have changed is the terminology: "outlining" is now called "pre-writing."

Teachers' Assessments of Related Factors

Policies alone do not determine teachers' decisions about curriculum. As they plan for instruction, teachers weigh several other factors in a rather subjective fashion. The most influential factors are these: test content; texts and other resources; student needs and interests; peer pressures; and curriculum guides. Teachers vary considerably in the weight they give to these factors. A major study of the planning of eighteen teachers indicated that they used one of four patterns of planning: six were "classic textbook followers"; six followed the text but were also strongly influenced by student differences; three were most influenced by district objectives; and three relied on past experiences (Schmidt, Porter, Floden, Freeman, and Schwille, 1987).

Test Content

State-developed assessment systems that hold teachers accountable for student achievement and use test results as a measure of achievement exert considerable pressure on the teacher to focus on the test. A six-state study by Porter, Smithson, and Osthoff (1994) of testing policies in mathematics and science led to three conclusions: testing is more controlling for elementary teachers than it is for secondary teachers; testing is more prevalent in mathematics than in science; and state testing programs are not always congruent with the state's curriculum reform agenda. Although the conventional wisdom holds that teachers resent the imposition of state testing mandates, Porter and his colleagues found that teachers in South Carolina (which had one of the most prescriptive policies) saw the state tests as a necessary evil. Finally, Darling-Hammond's review of the research on the impact of testing on instruction concluded that standardized test items strongly influenced teachers' choice of content and methodology.

Observe, however, that the impact of high-stakes tests on students may vary considerably. Cohen and Spillane (1994) suggest that such tests are more likely to affect poor and minority students, since more advantaged students pass the tests with minimal effort.

Texts and Other Resources

Although teachers are often perceived as driven by the textbook, the research indicates that they vary considerably in the attention they pay to the textbook. Since most elementary teachers teach the four academic subjects, they tend to rely more upon the text than do secondary teachers, who usually see themselves as subject-matter experts. Elementary teachers are more inclined to rely upon their prior experience and their knowledge of what works.

Cohen and Ball (1990) challenge the widely held belief that the uniform adoption of textbooks results in the standardization of content. They point out that teachers vary considerably in their use of the same text, especially if state guidelines are flexible about content. They conclude that textbooks are "rubbery agents of policy" (p. 251). Sykes (1990) reaches the same conclusion, noting that textbooks only imperfectly represent new approaches to curriculum. Cohen and Spillane (1994) observe that textbooks give teachers many choices about topics, enabling teachers to make choices about the content they cover.

Student Needs and Interests

In the Cornbleth (1995) study, teachers reported that their perceptions of students' needs were second only to the teachers' experience in determining what to teach. Teachers consider several student factors as they make long-term and short-term plans, as follows:

- Students' prior learning. ("They read parent-child stories last year; this year they can try writing one.")

- Students' learning needs. ("They should study vocabulary so they can do well on the SATs.")

- Students' awareness of external events. ("They'll be hearing about the comet; we should study it in science.")

- Students' abilities. ("They are an immature group; they should use manipulatives.")

- Student demographics. ("I must include some myths from other countries for the immigrant kids in that sixth-period class, so that they know I value diversity.")

With respect to this last factor, Cornbleth notes that California teachers seemed rather concerned with the changing demographics of the student population, as they reflected about students' needs.

Peer Pressures

Several years ago Silver (1973) pointed out that, because teachers work in isolation, they usually have peers but no colleagues. Even in a relatively cellular environment, however, teachers seem to influence each other in deciding what to teach. In one important study teachers reported that "other teachers' opinions" were one of six factors that influenced their curriculum decision making (Floden, Porter, Schmidt, Freeman, and Schwille, 1980). In many instances the influence of peers on such decisions is manifested in informal exchanges, not in formal faculty meetings.

Curriculum Guides

Despite the trust that curriculum leaders seem to place in curriculum guides as agents of policy, the evidence indicates that experienced teachers make only very general use of such guides. They tend to consult the guide briefly when the school year begins, to remind themselves of general district expectations. Clark (1986) concluded that after twenty months of curriculum meetings, teachers found a new guide to be too difficult to use and unlikely to be effective. As a consequence they responded to the guide with "creative nonuse."

Summary and Implications

The research reviewed above presents a general picture of how teachers receive and respond to state curriculum policies. The policies themselves are often ambiguous and contradictory. They pass through the filter of district and school administrators' biases. Thus, how teachers understand a policy is quite different from what the policy makers intended. Teachers then integrate their understanding of the new policy with their present practice, considering other factors as they do so. One of the most important factors affecting their decisions about content is the nature of high-stakes tests. Thus, teachers are active makers of policy-in-action who exert their own considerable influence.

These general findings suggest that classroom teachers do not see state policies as the bars in a narrow cell that limit their choices. Instead, they seem to view a new state policy as one more piece of furniture in an already crowded room.

The research, however, presents only a somewhat fuzzy collection of generalizations. The individual chapters that follow provide greater clarity and specificity, as individual teachers, representing several different states, speak personally about their own attitudes and practices.

References

Clandinin, D. J. 1986. *Classroom practice: Teacher images in action.* Philadelphia: Falmer.

Clark, P. C. 1986. *Classroom realities and creative nonuse.* Paper presented at annual meeting of the California Educational Research Association, Marina Del Rey (November). Education Document Reproduction Service Number ED 278 103.

Cohen, D. K. 1995. What is the system in systemic reform? *Educational Researcher,* 24 (10): 11-17, 31.

Cohen, D. K, and D. L. Ball.1990. Relations between policy and practice: A commentary. *Educational Evaluation and Policy Analysis,* 12: 249-256.

Cohen, D. K. and J. P. Spillane. 1994. Policy and practice: The relations between governance and instruction. In N. Cobb (Ed.), *The future of education: Perspectives on national standards in America*. New York: College Entrance Examination Board.

Cornbleth, C. 1995. Curriculum knowledge: Controlling the "great speckled bird." *Educational Review*, 47: 157-164.

Darling-Hammond, L. 1990. Instructional policy into practice: "The power of the bottom over the top." *Educational Evaluation and Policy Analysis*, 12: 233-241.

Elbaz, F. 1983. *Teacher thinking: A study of practical knowledge*. London: Croon Helm.

Floden, R. E., A.C. Porter, W. H. Schmidt, D. J. Freeman, and J. R. Schwille. 1980. *Response to curriculum pressures: A policy capturing study of teacher decisions about content*. East Lansing, Mich.: Institute for Research on Teaching, Michigan State University.

Noble, A. J., and M. L. Smith. 1994. *Old and new beliefs about measurement-driven reform: "The more things change, the more they stay the same."* Los Angeles, Calif.: National Center for Research on Evaluation, Standards, and Student Testing.

Porter, A.C., J. Smithson, and E. Osthoff, 1994. Standard setting as a strategy for upgrading high school mathematics and science. In R. F. Elmore and S. H. Fuhrman (Eds.), *The governance of the curriculum*, 138-166.

Schmidt, W. H., A.C. Porter, R. E. Floden, D. J. Freeman, and J. R. Schwille. 1987. Four patterns of teacher content decision-making. *Journal of Curriculum Studies*, 19: 439-455.

Silver, C. B. 1973. *Black teachers in urban schools*. New York: Praeger.

Sykes, G. 1990. Organizing policy into practice: Reactions to the cases. *Educational Evaluation and Policy Analysis*, 12: 243-247.

2

NEW YORK'S TEST-DRIVEN STANDARDS

by Jean Fontana

In New York state the word that best describes teachers' reactions to new curriculum standards, state tests, district mandates, and accountability initiatives of all kinds is "smug." Our smugness comes from teaching in a state that has had state-imposed Regents examinations since the Civil War era. This history causes us both individually and collectively to view externally-imposed standards with a punch-drunk, Rocky Balboa-type attitude of "hit me with everything you got, I can take it." And, like Rocky, we do take it in our stride, survive, and even triumph. What's more important, our students also learn to take it in their stride, survive, and triumph.

The Pressures of Tests, Standards, and Accountability

With all the changes occurring right now, teachers are facing several kinds of pressure—but most seem to be responding professionally to those pressures.

Tests, Tests, Tests

A *New York Times* reporter viewed newsworthy the fact that a student enrolled for 12 years in our public schools would take between 14 and 24 criterion-referenced state tests (Dao, 1994). As extraordinary as this number may seem, my colleagues and I consider it a low estimate because it takes into account only externally-imposed state tests and not standardized, norm-referenced achievement tests, intelligence tests, ubiquitous mid-terms and finals, and specific district testing programs. Typically, local district testing is quite extensive. Some districts require exit examinations from elementary to middle school; others require additional criterion-referenced testing of reading skills and the like. In fact, our students become so adept at taking tests that Cornell University researcher John Bishop believes that New York students are probably the best test takers in the nation (Shanker, 1995). Based on the sheer number of major tests they take, they should be.

It is this entrenched and prolific assessment system that drives instruction and accountability in our state. To use the vernacular of today's students, in New York tests rule!

Until 1999, New York had been testing third- and sixth-graders in math and reading for more than the 30 years I've been teaching. Material not covered on these tests was not taught until after the test was given, regardless of what any state syllabus or curriculum framework said. I submit, however, that this may not have been as bad as it sounds, for almost all of these state tests were planned, written, revised, assembled, and reviewed by statewide committees of classroom teachers. In fact, those teachers who made up the third- and sixth-grade math tests had to base each question on the state's math curriculum. According to Sandy Cohen, a retired elementary teacher who served on several of these test design committees, it was necessary to provide a page citation from the state's math syllabus for each question written.

Coupled with this committee's acute awareness of the direction that mathematics education was taking, this practice enabled committee members to embed some of the emerging math standards in the "old" math tests. Therefore, when the National Council of Teachers of Mathematics (NCTM), announced their national standards, third- and sixth-grade teachers in New York were not caught completely by surprise. We had already begun teaching our students in some of the areas and with the kinds of activities called for by the standards.

The rub here is that the job of creating new state tests other than secondary Regents exams has been contracted out to a commercial testing company. Although the rationale for doing this probably had something to do with the concept of faster and cheaper, the 8.4 million dollar contract with CTB/ McGraw-Hill (Hildebrand, 1999b), seems to belie this. Moreover, the loss of teacher involvement with teachers' curriculum acumen is frightening. Those of us in the field anticipated that the nitty-gritty changes in testing would include more writing, real-life problem-solving and performance tasks. We also realized that the grades in which students take exams would have to be changed to fourth and eighth, so that the state's program would be aligned with national guidelines. A few teachers expected that state tests would become more demanding; most others feared that in order to give everyone a fair chance of passing, something about the tests would be "dumbed down." A cursory examination of the new English language arts test that is now being given to fourth graders seems to indicate that the teachers were right. This new test requires that students be skilled not only in answering multiple choice comprehension questions but also in being able to synthesize reading material and then write responses based on that material. This part of the test measures listening skills that once were provided only by radio drama, coupled with note-taking abilities and writing skills par excellence. This is daunting certainly, but the elaborate, expensive marking process and the necessity for subjective judgments in grading the written response sections (even if specific rubrics are adhered to in the future) leave it open to criticism and controversy.

Standards Are Not the Driving Force

The sweeping action of the Board of Regents in adopting "new" standards in seven disciplines in 1996 should have indicated that these standards would become the impetus for curriculum, instruction, and accountability. And indeed our state education department quickly announced that new curriculum frameworks based on these standards were being written for the arts, English language arts, languages other than English, and social studies, as well as for several combined subjects: mathematics with science and technology; health with physical education and home economics; and career development with occupational studies. Unfortunately, some of the learning standards listed for these subject areas are not exactly brand new or demanding. Teachers have seen them before listed as curriculum goals, learning objectives, or student competencies. Furthermore, they are written in a style designed to irritate no one and are generally quite anemic.

As for the "new" curriculum frameworks, the one for third-grade social studies is essentially the old ho-hum curriculum repackaged with a new cover.

There are, however, two specific achievement standards that do provide a level of challenge in the English language arts core curriculum. Elementary students will be required to read 25 books per year and, beginning in second grade, write an average of 1,000 words or more per month across all content areas and standards. On those rare occasions when second- or third-grade teachers have spoken together as a group about these standards, the requirement of reading 25 books has appeared to be doable. On the other hand, meeting the thousand-word writing requirement in these early grades, they state with a wink and a sly smile, may require counting the repetitive copying of spelling words.

These teachers do, however, have a great deal more to say about the large number of hours that a documentation process called the Literacy Profile will take. This profile, as it is presently being presented, will require classroom teachers to complete individualized reading inventories and an in-depth analysis of writing samples for every student twice a year. This process would result in 12 pages of documentation per student. In a class of 25 that's 300 pages. It is not surprising, therefore, that teachers are outraged, for we know this will mean the loss of precious instructional time to assessment overkill.

What should be receiving anxious attention is the linkage of subjects. The current trend toward the integration of disciplines reflects the work of several national groups. This cross-subject integration should be causing the "purists" among us some consternation, but it's not because our focus is strictly on assessment. New York teachers will not acknowledge any need for change until standards and linkages are incorporated in tests. This is the only action that will proclaim to us the seriousness of our state's commitment and thus signal the direction instruction will take. New York State Education Commissioner Richard P. Mills understands this and recognizes the urgency in getting the new tests out so that "teachers will be able to say, 'I see now how my curriculum will have to change, how my practice will have to change. I see now how professional development has to be refocused'" (Ward, 1997, p. 12).

The commissioner's prayers will be answered, for he will get from teachers exactly what they perceive the tests require. But the commissioner may, as a Garth Brooks song says, be thankful for "some unanswered prayers." A committee that reviewed the results of the fourth-grade English language arts pilot test for one district recommended to teachers that, "students will need practice in determining main idea, cause and effect, etc., within shorter genres. Critical responses within a multiple choice test format need to be practiced for the short stories." I do not believe that an emphasis on piecemeal skill development is what our commissioner is praying for.

Big Changes and Confusing Consequences

A startling change that is part of the state's new assessment program deals with new standards and requirements for graduation. Currently, New York has a differentiated diploma system. In order to graduate from high school with a Regents-endorsed diploma, most college-bound secondary students take a sequence of rigorous Regents courses and must pass eight or nine Regents exams in these areas of concentration. The original intention of this testing program, which began in 1878, was to help the state colleges make admissions decisions. Special education students with severe handicaps can and will continue to earn Individualized Education Program (IEP) diplomas. Although other students could formerly earn a local, non-Regents-endorsed high school diploma by passing minimum competency tests, this will no longer be so. Competency tests are being phased out. By September 2001, all students who enter ninth grade will be required to pass at least five Regents exams in English, global studies, U.S. history, math, and science with a score of 65 or better in order to graduate. They will also earn a Regents diploma. The confusion caused by this new requirement, the resulting devaluation of the hallowed Regents diploma, and all the squabbling about diploma labels are all causing apoplexy for school superintendents like mine.

Teachers have always known that, to be effective, rigorous tests based on standards grounded in content must be linked to real consequences (Gandal, 1996). Not being able to graduate certainly is a real consequence, and from a teacher's perspective it also represents a new and long overdue focus—student accountability.

But our state's enduring emphasis on school-district accountability is not going to fade. In fact, greater attention is going to be paid to the results that individual schools have achieved in meeting the new assessment standards set by the Regents.

In order to do this, the New York State School Report Card was developed in 1996. Each report card shows test data enhanced by graphs about an individual school and compares these data with an average of the testing results of the entire district, similar schools in other districts, and all public schools in our state. The report card points out the number of students enrolled in a grade or subject in October and the number tested later in the school year. Data on minimum competency levels and mastery is also presented. The report card gives other information too: the school's enrollment; number of teachers, other professionals, and paraprofessionals; percentage of students eligible for free lunches or with limited English proficiency; expenditure per student; and attendance and suspension rates. Although testing data on students classified as handicapped were not originally included, this omission is now being corrected. New information continues to be added each year. The Regents Task Force on Teaching is even recommending that the number of teachers rated unsatisfactory should also be listed on each school's report card (New York State Board of Regents, 1998, p. 28).

In the past, schools that had at least 65 percent of their students scoring at or above minimum competency on state tests were considered to be doing a satisfactory job (No Excuses, 1996). Now the state requires that at least 90 percent of all students meet the minimum standards. Schools that are farthest from the state standards in reading or math or have a high drop-out rate, and also those that are considered most in need of improvement are placed on the list of schools under registration review—the SURR list. Out of the 4,167 public schools in our state, 2 percent have been judged to be failing. Of the 100 schools on the 1998 SURR list, 97 are in New York City. Each of these failing schools is given a tiny planning grant of about $5,000 and required to develop a corrective action plan. Sometimes the corrective action decided upon is to close and redesign the school. That is exactly what happened to 13 SURR schools in June 1996. They were then reopened that September with new identities. SURR schools that fail to make adequate progress within three academic years have their state registration revoked. In June 1997, James Monroe High School ceased to exist. With the higher requirements, state officials felt that the SURR list might swell, but it hasn't. In fact, the state was able to raise "... the minimum level of reading achievement used to identify SURR schools in New York City by as much as 10 percentage points" (New York State Education Department, 1997, p. 1).

New York's *modus operandi* has always been to make public the results of testing. The scores of the elementary and middle level testing programs, along with the results of the Regents exams, comprise the bulk of a superintendent's report on the state of his or her local school district to the board of education and community. Such reports are usually presented just before the budget vote is scheduled. Ultimate accountability!

Kids Fail/Teachers Remediated

In good financial times when additional funding is made available for school improvement projects and programs, such money is often earmarked for staff development. Will the skills and abilities of teachers continue to be viewed as the problem?

At the secondary level teachers have always been blamed for the percentage of students who fail. "The consequences although never officially spelled out or consistent are related in stories told in faculty rooms and at local [Teacher] Centers. Banishment from the high school, a full load of competency classes and the stigma of being regarded as a 'poor teacher' are just three of the punishments that teachers cite most often" (Fontana and Weinstein, 1990, p. 23).

At the elementary level the onus for student success or failure is placed on the teacher who administers the test, rather than on all those who have taught the child up to that point. Having a whole semester or year to prepare students for a test helps create this kind of one-teacher accountability. In the "old days" tests were scheduled in late September or early October. This timing gave classroom teachers just enough time to familiarize students with the test's style but not enough time to teach for the test. Then for some reason, the date for these tests was changed to later in the school year. The results were published in local newspapers, comparisons were made, and teaching for the test began.

When data from Long Island school report cards showing the results of third-graders' reading ability were published by the *New York Times* ("Report Card," 1997), my three colleagues and I went around patting each other on the back. We had worked as a team and our scores were terrific! We were congratulated by exactly two other people: Richard Maynard, a veteran teacher, stopped by each of our classrooms to tell us what a great job we had done, and our principal congratulated us at a grade-level meeting at which we were the only ones present. We tried to laugh this off, knowing the amount of attention we would have been given had the result been less than desirable. We also reminded ourselves that New York has never given a ticker-tape parade for teachers, even in years when we generated more than one-third of the 300 semifinalists in the Westinghouse (now Intel) science competition (Hildebrand, 1997, 1999a).

Isn't it amazing that teachers are never questioned about or recognized for good results!

How Teachers Survive and Triumph

One reason New York teachers are able to cope with superimposed standards, tests, the lack of recognition, and accountability programs of all kinds is that we are highly educated professionals. According to the statistics, 75.3 percent of us have at least a master's degree and 92.5 percent are either provisionally or permanently certified in the area or subject we teach (New York State Education Department, 1997-98). After a three-year probationary period, we enjoy the rights that tenure gives us with respect to due process and academic freedom, as well as the protection it provides from district politics. Tenure removes obstacles and ancillary concerns that might otherwise interfere with our focus. Teacher tenure is often a hot political issue in New York. Our former United States senator, Alfonse D'Amato, made tenure (along with teacher bashing) a campaign issue. We actively worked to defeat him, because New York teachers know that without tenure, outspoken teachers who uphold high academic standards with demanding homework loads, tough grading policies, and no-nonsense behavior standards—and especially those of us who attain high salary status or age—would be quickly replaced.

Most of us believe that teaching is a lifelong learning process. Even if we didn't, the way many districts structure salary increments (allowing for movement to higher steps based on additional college and in-service course credits) encourages teachers to continue taking courses beyond the master's degree (the basic requirement for permanent certification) and to participate in a variety of professional development activities. In spite of this capitalistic incentive, in 1998 our state created a continuing-education teacher certification requirement. Beginning September 1, 2000, newly hired teachers will be required to participate in 175 hours of in-service training every five years. I often wonder why so much time and energy were expended on creating this kind of compulsory continuing education, when it was obvious that this was exactly what a majority of New York teachers were already doing.

We teachers devote the first day of every school year to spelling out our own academic and behavior standards. Students, be they kindergartners or high school seniors, are made aware of exactly what we expect. And our students will often go to great lengths to meet what is expected of them. For example, one of our high school teachers, Mary Gough, who was from the "old school," insisted that students in her classes come dressed appropriately. She didn't care what they wore elsewhere, but in her classroom there would be decorum—no shorts or scanty tops. Outside her classroom the scene of kids hopping into sweatshirts and pants to cover whatever was bare was a sight to behold.

Now we have to incorporate additional external standards into our own repertoire. As stated, in those subject areas and grades that are tested, it will, of course, be the content of the new state tests that will determine what will actually be taught. Many teachers, including me, keep copies of old, nonsecure state tests and flip though them periodically, checking to see if we are on target. Unfortunately for us test collectors, copies of the state's 1999 English language arts test were collected, counted, and sent back to the state to be destroyed, in spite of the fact that some of the test's reading passages were known prior to testing, had been read by some students using a certain reading series, and were readily available on the Internet (Hildebrand, 1999b).

As for adapting the curriculum to the demands of a standardized test, I have never seriously considered doing this. To do so would seem to defeat its purpose.

In subject areas that are not tested, teachers will use with judicious selectivity both state frameworks and district curriculum guides to see if what is being planned is consistent with these publications. State frameworks are usually skimpy on content but heavy on skill development, student attitudes, teaching strategies, and relevant classroom applications often described in what E. D. Hirsch calls "abstract, pseudotechnical jargon" (Core Knowledge, 1996, p. 5). District curriculum guides are a little better, having been developed by a committee of teachers who customarily work on them over the summer. Regrettably, the guides are usually distributed with no explanation from those who have painstakingly created them.

Planning, Teaching, and Coping

Documenting what I believe to be true about how teachers try to cope with the latest educational initiative may not be the smartest way for me to survive as a teacher or maintain friendly relationships with those in other positions, but it does enable me to keep standard operating practices and other accompanying absurdities in perspective.

For instance, I'm supposed to worry about the days that I select to give tests, conduct performance assessments, or plan special activities like field trips or the presentation of plays. You see, I've received a copy of "A Calendar of Religious Holidays and Ethnic Festivals," which I believe originally came from another school district, along with an actual directive from an assistant superintendent to "please make note of these dates to ensure that testing or other special events are not scheduled. . . ." I've counted these days, and in order to comply with this directive I would have to avoid almost 100 days in the 184-day school year. Is this reasonable?

As a teacher I deal with such lunacy daily—and I teach in a good school district. Is it any wonder, then, that the incongruity between critical reasoning approaches and rote learning doesn't faze me? In fact, I happily mix modes of inquiry such as concept formation and attainment models, reciprocal teaching, cooperative learning, role playing, Synectics, and higher-level thinking strategies right along with choral and oral reading, recitation of the times tables, spelling lists, textbook-centered lessons, and drill and practice sheets. Although I am a proponent of a literature-rich reading program, I don't faint at the mention of phonics. My reading lessons are just as likely to be based on selections from a basal reader as they are on "chapter books," plays, poems, songs, math problems, directions for a game, various kinds of schedules, newspaper articles and cartoons, or a film. I model and teach the writing process, and yet, in assigning topics that enable me to integrate writing into other subject areas, I give specific guidelines as to how many words should make up a typical sentence, and how many sentences should be written.

This very scary ability I've developed to think and work in this illogical way, to schedule and plan around obstacles, and to view pull-outs and constant interruptions as normal, leads me to conclude that "insanity" is definitely contagious. Teachers like me not only catch it from our own children but also from our students, whose abilities, styles of learning, and needs dictate instructional approaches. We also catch it from administrators, who catch it from central office, who catch it from the state education department, who catch it from. . .

Helping Students Survive and Triumph

Students in our state do not become adept at taking tests solely through exposure. New York teachers make sure that their students become familiar with testing situations and skilled in the procedures involved.

In the past, third graders were taught early that, when in doubt about an answer on a multiple-choice question, they should stick with their first choice. Fifth graders could give workshops on the steps involved and the kind of sequencing words used when writing "how to" paragraphs for the writing test. Sixth graders understood that in order to get the highest possible score on the essay questions for the social studies test, they needed to choose a topic that was covered most recently in sixth grade, rather than one that was covered last year by the fifth-grade curriculum. Needless to say, the training of elementary students in the skills necessary for the new tests is well under way.

Secondary students use Regents Review Books, which contain past Regents exams. Although teachers can't officially require students to purchase these books, they strongly urge them to do so. Students who do not purchase such books borrow copies that the teacher has purchased. Although Regents Review Books are used only in New York state, they generate millions of dollars in sales.

Yes, we teachers do spend a great deal of time preparing students to take tests. And yes, our students become smart, savvy, skilled test-takers. In fact, they have "the highest average SAT scores" in the nation (A System of High Standards, 1996, p. 25). Could we do any less and be fair to them or ourselves when this is the major criterion upon which we are judged?

How One District Is Responding

Sometimes just setting high standards makes things improve. This was the case recently when a Long Island school district was required to use the new Regents graduation standards to try to "reinvent" itself.

On January 3, 1996, the New York State Board of Regents in an unprecedented action seized control of the Roosevelt Public School District by removing its duly elected school board from office. The state legislature had made provisions for doing this, and the takeover did not come without repeated warnings and, finally, an ultimatum from Commissioner of Education Mills. The Board was replaced by an Oversight Panel, chaired by Dr. Daniel Domenech.

The troubled school system had been on the state's SURR list of low-performing schools since 1990. As a result, the Oversight Panel had been involved in the district prior to the state's official takeover and had developed a blueprint for fixing the schools which "the Board had refused to follow" (Sandberg, 1996, p. 11). Only two students of 116 graduates in 1995 earned a Regents diploma—versus a "local" diploma—for passing the state's more rigorous Regents tests. As Gray (1996) noted, "That represented the lowest Regents graduation rate of 120 districts with high schools (on Long Island). . . . Regents courses were virtually nonexistent."

In the 1996 Oversight Panel Report, Domenech concluded as follows:

> Twenty years of neglect and poor management had taken its toll on the schools and the community. . . . Constant turnover in the district's hierarchy fostered a lack of continuity in programs and administrative practices. School facilities . . . had become hazardous firetraps. The lack of textbooks and instructional supplies and materials had seriously hampered the teaching and learning process. The district's finances were in disarray, complicated by a substantial budget deficit (New York State Education Department, 1996, p. 3).

Standards Aid Survival

Before the takeover, in September 1995, the Oversight Panel had mandated that Roosevelt High School become an all-Regents school. David Carroll, who was then president of the Roosevelt Teachers Association, felt that the Regents mandate combined with the takeover was key in providing some positive actions. Carroll stated, "Teachers were finally supplied with textbooks and given tremendous in-service opportunities which were received very enthusiastically. Over 120 teachers were involved in training over the summer. Curriculum was written. Yes, it was the exposure to the Regents. . ." (D. Carroll, personal communication, October, 1996.)

In June 1995, before the Regents mandate, only 12 students took Regents exams in just English and French (New York State Education Department, 1996, p. 22). In 1996, as a result of the requirement that all students take Regents courses and exams, 964 exams were taken and 321 were passed (p. 22). For the first time in a long time, students took Regents in sequential math 1, 2, and 3, American history, global studies 2, biology, earth science, chemistry, Spanish, and occupational studies (p. 22). Although the failure rate was unacceptable, this represented a dramatic change.

Veteran teacher Jannie West's faith in the system was restored by the state's actions, but she wonders why the slaughter of standards was allowed in the first place. "A former superintendent just did away with all the Regents courses."

Much of the credit for the initial changes goes to Michael Mostow, the state-appointed executive director, who was in charge of the day-to-day operations of the district. Carroll said Mostow was "unique," high praise from a union leader. According to Carroll, "Mostow was into shared decision making and teacher input and he practiced what he preached—a major difference."

But then Mostow left to become a superintendent in another district, and the momentum slowed. Carroll described the situation that followed as a "state of paralysis" and Domenech stated that progress had come to "a screeching halt" (Sandberg, 1997, p. 3). They both blamed the situation on the newly elected school board's inability to set priorities and make timely decisions. Their emotional reaction to this setback, however, was significant, for this was a school district that no one was supposed to care about. Obviously, these two leaders cared; teachers and community members cared too. People cared so much that even a quick fix like the Edison Project was seriously considered for awhile.

Carroll has retired, but Mostow returned to Roosevelt as superintendent of schools. The new union president, Charlene Stroughn, and teachers are optimistic, but they recognize that Roosevelt still has a long way to go.

One area that both teachers and serious students would like to see strengthened is discipline. A math teacher laments, "How can I be responsible for what my students are learning when they can come into class whenever they want? This disturbs everyone." A student at a Regents review session at the local PAL (Police Athletic League) center states, "I can't concentrate on the lesson that's being presented in one section of the room when there's a show going on in the other."

Roosevelt is trying to solve a multitude of problems that have plagued this district for a very long time. One action is not going to end its troubles, but if all these talented people continue to listen to each other's ideas, Roosevelt could still reinvent itself.

Prerequisites for Success: A Teacher's Perspective

In spite of my cynical rhetoric and critical scrutiny of the standards movement, I support rigorous, challenging, achievable standards. Teachers always have. And as Glatthorn points out in the introductory chapter of this book, teachers are active makers of policy-in-action who exert their own considerable influence. But, no matter how badly we may want the standards movement to succeed, we know that we can't do it alone. The support of administrators and parents is vital. In addition to this, there are also several other prerequisites, including effective teaching, parent involvement, relationships with higher education, good communication, and sufficient resources.

Create an Awareness of Effective Teaching Practices

A goodly number of administrators, even those who have been teachers for short periods of time, give the impression that they do not understand our craft. It is, therefore, essential that school administrators be trained to recognize what constitutes effective teaching practice. Such a lack of understanding can't continue to coexist with demanding standards.

A colleague developed a great directed reading/thinking activity (DRTA) lesson using a historical document. Each year she resurrects this lesson and uses it with her new class of elementary students. Most historians, especially our New York State archivists, would applaud her efforts, for they actively encourage the study of history as it unfolds from such documents. Unfortunately, she forgot that she had used this lesson several years ago for a "show and tell" type observation. When she repeated it for a recent observation by the same administrator, she was lambasted for doing "the same old thing," rather than praised.

A middle-school principal countermanded one of my homework assignments because this principal felt it was too difficult for sixth graders. Since we were going to study ancient Rome, I had decided to rip up an adult-type coloring book that had pictures of Roman artifacts—chariots, clothing, legions' equipment—and have my students work on them over the December recess. They were also given a list of old movies that they could watch, which I believed would help in building their background knowledge about the period. While admonishing me for doing this, the principal pointed out that this was their vacation, and besides, those coloring pictures were much too difficult. This principal could have legitimately criticized my assignment because of its "history according to Hollywood" slant. This, however, was never mentioned.

These are not atypical incidents. Teachers often regale each other with stories about the following oft-repeated scenario. The administrator arrives unannounced at the classroom door prepared to observe the teacher. Upon discovering that the teacher is busy (distributing or retrieving materials, cleaning up a messy project, disciplining a student, or just watching the interactions of those children working by themselves in cooperative groups), the administrator states aloud that he or she will come back another day when the teacher is really teaching.

Part of the problem may be that administrators perceive teaching literally as a "stand-up" act involving the whole class or a large group. Teachers know, however, that it is more often a ground-level, close, personal interchange.

Get and Keep Parents on Board

Parents need to understand that high standards are good not only for other children but also for theirs. Their input must be sought in order to develop a set of common expectations that they will accept and support. Although we teachers do not relish the persistent presence of parents in our classrooms and schools, we must learn to view and accept them as partners in the education of their children.

We therefore need report cards that actually report to parents about students' academic abilities, not just about their effort. Recently, a student entered third grade with a glowing report card, but he couldn't decode one word. Based on this child's second-grade report card, his parents could have assumed that he was making normal progress. The pervasive proliferation of "feel good" developmental report cards does not serve the best interest of the child. Neither does the wholesale abandonment of ability-level grouping or grade placement based solely on age. Research indicates that retention does not work, but specially designed catch-up classes might. In my district extended readiness classes help primary students, who are not quite ready for the pressures of a first-grade class, prepare for reentry into a regular academic program by third grade.

Gandal (1996) points out, "Teachers who try to uphold high academic standards . . . are often pressured by administrators, parents, and students to ease up" (p.7). Teachers need to help everyone—especially parents—understand academic conventions. When one of my students scored only a 70 on a weekly spelling quiz, I wrote across the top of her paper, "Awful." Her parents immediately fired off a page-and-a-half letter, letting me have it. Didn't I know that I could ruin her self-esteem and that I should only give positive reinforcement? Nonsense! Could I have used a different word? Of course! I'm a writer and know several more tempered words. But I'm first and foremost a teacher and a grade of 70 preceded by grades of 100, 90, and 93 is awful. There is no other word. It sums up perfectly my assessment of her performance. Since she scored 100 on the next test, I believe she and her parents got my message. I did write a lengthy response to them about the concept of "earned self-esteem" but a former principal, Reno Calabrese, taught me that it's okay to respond but sometimes wiser not to mail the response. I'm not always smart enough to follow his advice, but in this case I did.

In an effort to console anxious parents about their child's poor performance on a state or district test, guidance counselors, administrators, and teachers, too, will tell parents not to worry because the scores are "only one indication of the child's performance and ability on one particular day." So are the results of the U.S. presidential election. Just try consoling the loser with that statement. We must all forbid the telling of such lovely lies.

An extensive longitudinal study of 20,000 secondary students by Steinberg, Brown, and Dornbusch (1996) points out that too many students do not take their education seriously. These researchers have concluded that the only way to "reengage" students is to affect the forces in their lives outside of school (p. 194). It is, therefore, crucial that parents become our allies and we theirs.

Establish Authentic Relationships

There are presently far too many researchers who have not discovered how to examine our profession. Although there are also notable exceptions, I'd like to suggest something that is obviously missing that might help remedy this situation. Just try engaging teachers, especially those who are not immediately propelled to the forefront by administrators, in simple two-way conversation. Cold, clinical interviews, observations, and surveys do not encourage teachers to help researchers focus their efforts on areas of real concern rather than on peripherals. Nor do they allow us to correct misperceptions. Two-way conversations might. Perhaps if a well-known researcher had engaged in such two-way conversations with teachers, he would not have recommended the study of the shortening of "opening exercises" and "clean-up" activity time as a collaborative challenge for teachers and administrators. By talking with teachers, he would have learned that this is perhaps their least pressing concern. They could have saved him the embarrassment of printing such an insipid, time-consuming suggestion in his book. No wonder teachers tune out researchers. We need meaningful insight into the practice and improvement of our profession.

Real partnerships also need to be nurtured with members of the department or school of education at local colleges and universities. It would be interesting to see if a relationship similar to the hospital-medical school model could be developed.

But first we need to understand each other and the way schools really operate. I remember attending a small dinner meeting at a local university, at which Bruce Joyce was the guest of honor. When the conversation turned to peer coaching, I blurted out that teachers often share effective lessons with student teachers and colleagues prior to formal observations. I added that veteran teachers have even helped student teachers and first-year novices package and practice these "show and tell" lessons. This *faux pas* on my part was at first met with deadly silence—then outrage—from university supervisors. I also know of teachers who warn their students that, when any lesson is being observed by a professor or school administrator that there will be zero tolerance of any student misbehavior. Students must appear to be enraptured by everything presented. Does any observer of such performances ever wonder why no student has to go to the lavatory or nurse's room, or why no student ever has to go to the library, or why no one ever passes a note or elbows a neighbor during this performance?

Improve Communication

While it may be believed that teachers learn about new policies, curriculum initiatives, or changes in testing practices through educational channels, the truth is that we usually learn things right along with everyone else, through the public media.

For example, in 1996, New York Governor George Pataki spearheaded the passage of a law that required teaching about the potato famines in Ireland. At the time there were sensationalized stories in the newspapers about how young students would now have to be "burdened" with lessons about these potato famines. The concerns of outraged political commentators were heard on both radio and television. They considered this an inappropriate invasion by a powerful political group into the curriculum, which they seemed to regard as sacred and non-political. In spite of all this hoopla, or maybe because of it, at the time of this writing teachers have yet to receive any kind of directive from anyone in education about teaching this to our students. If a directive ever comes, we'll teach it. As experienced teachers, we'll figure out just where, when, and how to cram this into the curriculum. It won't be the first time we've been asked to manipulate the curriculum in this way. This teacher, however, is anxiously awaiting the day that I receive a directive from anyone stating that it's all right to take something out.

Right now, State Education Commissioner Mills would benefit from an official two-way communication channel, for I believe he is making a blunder that teacher-conversations might help him avoid. You see, he is putting three state tests for elementary school children into fourth grade. This is not a good idea, no matter what the national guidelines suggest. One state test per grade level is doable; two are masochistic. As a third-grade teacher, I can state this with certainty. Three, however, will kill the joy of teaching and learning, and could lead to a teacherless grade. My high school colleagues would also like to point out that the devaluation of the Regents' diploma may cause an exodus from eleventh grade to college teaching.

Secure Resources for Remediation

When a student works for a passing grade and achieves it, the victory should be sweet and celebrated. But failure must also be recognized and remediated. Therefore, along with higher standards, teachers need the commitment of resources for remediation that will help, not hinder, them. Federal and state projects that give money to schools for this purpose must allow for real instructional flexibility. The present provision that remediation "supplement, not supplant" and yet be congruent with local core programs is oxymoronic. It may make sense in Washington, D.C., or in Albany, New York (many strange things do), but it doesn't make sense when a classroom teacher is always missing several students because they are pulled out, or worse, pulled aside for remediation. One year, four of my students received one hour and twenty minutes of additional instruction in reading and math three days a week at the most inopportune times. They became so confused and actually resented these sessions because they were missing so much in other subject areas such as science and social studies. A colleague in a city school system complains that she must spend one out of five days documenting remediation instead of providing it. "We are told to put the kids on the computer for 'computer-aided instruction,' so that we can do the paperwork."

Will the Standards Movement Survive and Triumph?

Implementation of national standards has already brought a renewed interest in the importance of plain old knowledge, a sorely neglected category. At some point it will also bring renewed emphasis on instruction and teachers.

But even an instructional imperative will not mean that teachers will have top priority at the copy machine or that the rooms in which lessons are taught and tested in New York State will be air-conditioned, as are those rooms where administrators and their secretaries work. That's too much to ask. It could, however, mean access to 19th century technology, like a phone. Imagine a school where 37 elementary teachers no longer have to share the one and only phone designated for their use! It could also mean some old-fashioned window screens, so we won't have to spend instructional time battling the daily invasion of bees in some of our classrooms.

In order to have the greatest impact, however, this newest panacea must mean that teachers will be backed by those at all levels of administration in upholding high academic and behavioral standards. It must mean that the voices of primary teachers are heard when they lobby for a particular reading series that just happens to have a strong phonics component, even when phonics is not in vogue. It must mean that books that teachers choose to use remain uncensored and that computer programs are not purged under the guise of "security concerns." Academic freedom must be reborn. Furthermore, it must mean that teachers have adequate support to help them with any students with special needs in their classes so that they can devote full time to curriculum requirements.

Success in meeting standards will require open, dialogue-rich collaboration about common expectations—"two-way" conversations. We have heard this said before about other initiatives. Maybe those innovations were abandoned because such dialogues never occurred.

So get ready to sit up straight, put your feet on the floor under the desk, and begin paying close attention to all the voices coming from the classroom. Because if this is not done, then the standards movement will be just another "same old, same old." It will run the usual seven years, as do most "new" programs, all the while dying from terminal lip service.

But even if this happens and the movement toward strong standards fizzles, don't mourn for the Rocky Balboas of education. We teachers will continue coping as always with every punch that is thrown. It's the nature of the fighter in us. We'll dodge, weave, and dazzle with our footwork. We'll get knocked down because our gloves are "low bid" or our corner lacks continuous and strong support. But it will be our smugness and tenacity that will enable us to keep getting up just before the count of ten. For in spite of all the shots to our heads, we know that schools evolved from teachers and not the other way around (Meade, 1985). We just have to continue slugging it out while waiting for everybody else to finally catch on.

References

A system of high standards: What we mean and why we need it. 1996. *American Educator*, 20 (1): 22-27.

Core knowledge schools take root across the country. 1996. *American Educator*, 20 (4): 4-7.

Dao, J. 1994. New York State is reshaping testing system for schools. *New York Times*, April 30.

Fontana, J. E., and S. G. Weinstein. 1990. Teachers centers: Finally a bandwagon for teachers. *NYSASCD impact on instructional improvement*, 23 (3): 22-25.

Gandal, M. 1996. *Making standards matter 1996*. Washington, D.C.: American Federation of Teachers.

Gray, K. 1996. A class act. *Newsday*, June 20.

Hildebrand, J. 1997. Eyes on prize. *Newsday*, January 14.

Hildebrand, J. 1999a. Research winners. *Newsday*, January 12.

Hildebrand, J. 1999b. Probe of 4th-grade test cheating. *Newsday*, January 15.

Meade, E. J. Jr. 1985. *Forward in teacher development in schools: A report to the Ford Foundation*. New York : Academy for Educational Development.

New York State Board of Regents. 1998. *Teaching to Higher Standards: New York's Commitment*, July. Albany, N.Y.: Author.

New York State Education Department. 1996. *Oversight panel report Roosevelt Union Free School District. Long Island, New York*. Albany, N.Y.: Author.

New York State Education Department. 1997-98. *Basic educational data system master file*. Albany, N.Y.: Author.

No excuses: schools must succeed, or else. 1996. *Newsday*, November 17.

Report card: How the island's 3rd graders measure up. 1997. *New York Times*, January 5.

Sandberg, B. 1996. Regents remove Roosevelt board. *New York Teacher*, January 22.

Sandberg, B. 1997. Administrative drift imperils Roosevelt. *New York Teacher*, January 27.

Shanker, A. 1995. Where we stand: Feeding and weighing. *New York Times*, April 9.

State education department removes eighteen New York public schools from registration review. 1997. *Newsletter of the Board of Education*, November 12.

Steinberg, L., B. B. Brown, and S. Dornbusch. 1996. *Beyond the classroom*. New York: Simon and Schuster.

Ward, D. 1997. The latest on standards. *New York Teacher*, January 27.

3

VOICES FROM A NATIVE AMERICAN CLASSROOM IN NEBRASKA

by Katherine Bauer-Sanders

When I began teaching on the Winnebago Indian Reservation in the fall of 1991, I had the advantage of being a parent as well as a teacher. As a parent, I appreciated the significance of individuality. I was aware of the possible consequences of comparing children's abilities, interests, and aptitudes. As children and parents entered my classroom, they were informed of the philosophy that would drive my teaching practice. A colorful poster adorned our doorway: "Kindergarten is a garden of children. Mrs. Sanders is our gardener. A good gardener does not expect all the flowers to bloom at the same time." The powers-that-be in my district enjoyed the poster and claimed to share the sentiment. In the spring of 1992, however, these kindred spirits mandated the administering of standardized tests at the kindergarten level. I reluctantly created the unnatural atmosphere dictated by standardized testing procedures. My heart was broken, but my spirit was not. I spent the better part of the following summer and the beginning of my second school year trying to persuade those decision makers that comparing children through standardized tests was neither objective, valid, or reliable, nor in the best interest of our children (Chambers, 1993; Harmon, 1989). I became quite versed in explaining the standard deviations and the distribution of scores within that infamous bell curve. I was unwilling to believe that 68 percent of my students could be classified average with approximately 5 percent either excelling or failing (Eichelberger, 1989).

In the spring of 1993, kindergarten was exempt from standardized tests! As much as my ego would have liked to credit my persistence and rhetoric, these were hardly the deciding factors. The individual writing-draft books, the then-meager checklist of basic skills, and the published works of my students (when compared with the language arts composite scores on the children's standardized tests) had proven beyond a shadow of a doubt that our standardized tests had no validity! I came to the realization that one individual could indeed impact on educational policies.

Building Local Standards

After research and authentic assessment results had spared my kindergartners from standardized testing procedures, I was ecstatic when our community decided to create district standards for education and the evaluation tools for those standards. Parents everywhere are concerned with their children and their education; parents on the reservations are no exception. The people of Winnebago love their children, have high aspirations, and make a commitment to problem-solving as opposed to finger-pointing. Community agencies, led by the joint efforts of the tribal council and the

Winnebago public school board, hired an educational consultant to coordinate community efforts to improve the educational systems in the preschools, the public and parochial schools, and the community college.

Using the National Educational Goals 2000 as well as the priorities and goals of the Indian Nations at Risk Task Force, the Winnebago community began the curriculum revision.

Subject area curriculum teams were organized and divided into smaller groups addressing the specific curriculum competencies for mathematics, science, social studies, language arts, physical education, the arts, and Winnebago language and culture. Since I was conducting graduate research in reading instruction, I requested the opportunity to work with the language arts competencies. Using various teaching resources, error analysis information from previous testing methods, and a formal knowledge of child development, school staff worked with parents to design a curriculum that would help students meet the challenges of being contributing members of the reservation community while competing successfully in a global society. Language arts competencies in the early elementary grades were categorized into reading, writing, listening, speaking, and thinking skills. Those skills were further divided into competencies for four year olds in the tribal Head Start program, five to six year olds in kindergarten, and six to seven year olds in the first grade.

We were mandated to categorize the competencies by grade level. The quandary this posed for me was defining a skill as first- or second-grade, or kindergarten. How was it determined that a book was a first-grade or a third-grade level book? Who or what determined that adding "ing" to words was a kindergarten or a first-grade skill? I realized that many competencies were prerequisites. Learning to read was dependent on discrimination skills, letter-to-sound connections, and other factors. Mathematics required a more defined hierarchy of standards based on logic, not grade level or age. If I could concentrate on building these necessary prerequisites, the task of taking children from where they were to where they needed to be would be based on developmental standards, rather than on artificially contrived grade-level standards. Without exception, the most difficult and time-consuming decisions made by our curriculum committee were not what the standards should be, but to which grade level they should be assigned.

An additional concern of mine regarded student advancement. When a child advanced a grade level, would the assumption be that he or she had successfully attained all of the competencies within that grade level? Defining standards by grade level might imply that teachers were accountable for competencies only within their grade level. What documentation measures would be instituted to prevent this situation from harming our children? Despite these unresolved concerns, the competency drafts were submitted to the educational consultant for evaluation and compilation into a single curriculum guide.

Observing the New Zealand Approach

The summer of 1995 afforded me the opportunity to study national standards in Auckland, New Zealand. Since we had completed our school's competency drafts only weeks before, this overseas study could not have occurred at a more opportune time. This was an independent study in natural language learning and a comparative study of Native Americans and Maoris and their respective educational systems.

Educators and administrators at Kauriland and Royal Road Schools in Auckland shared instructional strategies, methods and materials, authentic assessment tools, and detailed reporting methods. New Zealand's national standards, as developed by the ministry of education, guided instruction using detailed checklists of blended standards, as opposed to grade-level standards. In the first three levels of formal instruction, New Zealand educators were not as concerned with the year a skill was acquired as that it actually was acquired. Their standards checklists were the equivalent of the Winnebago competencies, but were much more detailed. These standards were divided into the following proficiency levels: pre-emergent, emergent, early, and fluent literacy. The standards were listed on student report forms and were used as American schools would use conventional report cards, with one major difference. Rather than a different report card being issued each year, a single report form followed the child through the first several years of school. The report form was marked with a different color ink each school year and used the following notations rather than letter grades: "not yet" was indicated with a small dot in the middle of the appropriate box on the grid; "beginning mastery" was indicated with a slash ($/$); "mastery" was indicated with an (X); and "mastered with confidence" was indicated with a vertical line through the X ($\mathbf{X}$). This made for easy longitudinal measurement. These sequential reports provided parents with concrete, comprehensive information specifically documenting their child's progress. The reports were also accompanied by a brief narrative regarding each child's level of cooperation, socialization, and attitude. Ongoing evaluation of student progress was shared with parents, administrators, and children.

Running records, an assessment of reading behaviors, were taken periodically and were used to evaluate the gradual progress that standardized tests could not measure. The reliability of running record scores for accuracy and error was 0.90 (Clay, 1995a). These assessments were evaluated and recorded on each child's permanent file. As all the instructional reading materials were leveled by various degrees of support and challenge, rather than by grade level, the evaluation of running records aided the teacher in providing the appropriate level of challenge in reading instruction. The running records, coupled with leveled reading materials, provided an authentic, valid, reliable, objective, and, more importantly, manageable system to document achievement and decisively meet instructional needs (Clay, 1995b).

Piloting District Standards

My research in New Zealand had addressed my concerns with grade-level competencies and documentation. During the pilot year of 1995-1996, my goals were to address the issues of parent involvement and documentation of our competency standards. Using the documentation techniques shared by the Auckland teachers, I elaborated on the Winnebago curriculum standards. My administrators allowed me to supplement the district reports and competencies, on the condition that all local standards would be addressed. Another victory! I was allowed to institute the blending of kindergarten through second-grade curriculum standards for language arts and mathematics. I was also allowed to incorporate additional standards to more closely monitor small learning steps and plan new learning (Daniels, 1996). My justifications were:

1) better planning for individual instruction that challenged every learner,
2) more complete understanding for parents, and
3) better communication between grade-level teachers.

This aided in planning instructional activities that challenged every child. Parents were enlightened with regard to the competencies required for emergent and early readers and writers. The scope and sequence of skills not only emphasized the necessary foundations and understandings, but indirectly stressed the importance of consistent attendance. Kindergarten attendance would be viewed as vital, given the scope and sequence of the competencies to be mastered. Our kindergarten work was now validated by our ability to document exactly what skills were valued. The other advantage of blended curriculum standards was a checklist that could easily follow children from one grade level to another, as well as one teacher to another. With consistent standards between grade levels, children were able to continue a developmentally appropriate educational program based on objective checklists of skills, rather than subjective letter grades or standardized test scores.

These individual checklists were color-coded by grade level, kindergarten through second grade. Each grade-level teacher was assigned a different color ink so individual student progress could be tracked by grade level. Maintaining color-coded checklists of competencies also addressed the issue of teacher accountability. Children could not be carelessly passed from grade level to grade level without parents and schools addressing the issue of student learning. The purpose was not to lay blame, but to improve instructional outcomes. Teachers could be assigned to compatible grade levels or team-teaching situations, thus utilizing teaching strengths. Students could be identified for special services and early intervention programs. Using checklists aided students in self-evaluation practices. Even kindergarten children could follow simple checklists in evaluating personal progress. Several times each year, students completed a self-evaluation form. Students were asked to identify what was most difficult for them, what was easiest for them, and what was a learning priority. To my amazement, nearly all the children selected as our next priority the same skill or competency I had identified!

Addressing parenting issues was my second goal that pilot year, because the community had cited parenting skills as the number one priority for our junior high and high school students. I chose to address parental concerns through parent meetings, family programs, and printed materials designed to inform, inspire, and involve families in the education process. Information sessions were held prior to kindergarten entry to stress the importance of attendance, participation by children and their families, involvement in decision making and program planning, and celebration of even the smallest learning steps. It was during these pre-kindergarten informational meetings that district standards were presented and explained. Parents were encouraged to share concerns, criticisms, or comments regarding the implementation of these standards. At this meeting, I made the commitment that information would be exchanged through parent letters, student-author's teas, musical presentations, class dramatizations, parties for families, and homework projects.

Several weeks into the school year, I responded to parent inquiries regarding the explanation of the reading and writing processes. Parents felt they could better understand the competencies if they understood the developmental processes involved in early literacy instruction. Parents were invited to after-school workshops explaining the checklists for emergent, early, and fluent readers and writers. Examples of developmental spelling were examined and their value as tools for evaluating what children did know was stressed. I wanted parents to realize that we were not reinventing spelling conventions, but rather were using a child's spelling to determine where that child was academically. I wanted parents to appreciate their own value as their children's first and foremost teachers and my greatest source of information, support, and constructive criticism.

It was during one of these information-sharing meetings that the concerns regarding accountability, lesson planning, and standardized testing were discussed. Parents wanted a reporting system that was specific, that reflected what their children had accomplished, and that addressed what their children were striving for during the upcoming quarter. In response to these concerns, I devised an assessment tool to gather base-line data on each child during the first month of school entry. Figure 3.1 shows a one-month checklist for mathematics. The information recorded on such a checklist would not only be used for a comparative assessment in the spring, but it would also guide the planning of a child's individual instructional program.

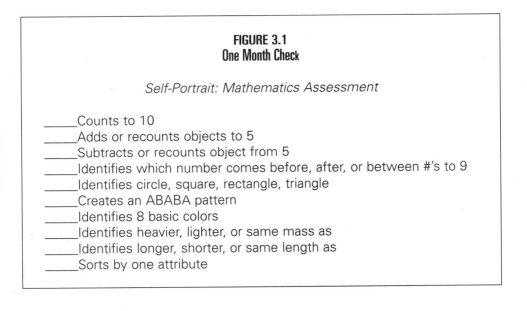

FIGURE 3.1
One Month Check

Self-Portrait: Mathematics Assessment

_____Counts to 10
_____Adds or recounts objects to 5
_____Subtracts or recounts object from 5
_____Identifies which number comes before, after, or between #'s to 9
_____Identifies circle, square, rectangle, triangle
_____Creates an ABABA pattern
_____Identifies 8 basic colors
_____Identifies heavier, lighter, or same mass as
_____Identifies longer, shorter, or same length as
_____Sorts by one attribute

FIGURE 3.2
Observations: Handedness, Attendance, Attitude, Curiosity, Motor Skills, etc.

Writing Assessment

_____Displays writing-like behavior
_____Dictates stories
_____Establishing directionality
_____Copies letters, words, and sentences
_____Writes using random letters
_____Writes using initial sounds
_____Writes using final sounds
_____Uses spaces between words
_____Begins with a capital letter
_____Ends with a full stop (.)

Concepts of Print

_____Shows real interest in books
_____Listens to stories being read aloud
_____Shows front and back of book
_____Realizes print contains a message
_____Uses picture to tell story in own words
_____Demonstrates knowledge of proper directionality
_____Has voice-print-point match
_____Attends to left page before right
_____Identifies letter and a word
_____Corresponds upper and lower case letters
_____Identifies first and last word on a page
_____Recognizes some high frequency words
_____Recognizes similarities in words
_____Relies on memory for reading
_____Uses picture cues
_____Uses semantic cues
_____Uses syntactic cues
_____Uses pragmatic cues
_____Uses text & pictures to sample, predict, confirm
_____Retells stories
_____Reads with expression
_____Selects appropriate reading material

Letter Identification Assessment

A F K P W Z B H O J U C Y

L Q M D N S X I E G R V T

a f k p w z b h o j u c y

l q m d n s x i e g r v t

The issue of teacher accountability for student learning would also be addressed. Base-line data would provide documentation of student growth for administrators, parents, myself, and, most important, for my students. Figure 3.2 is a summary of the base-line information collected for writing.

Each student was assigned a writing-draft book and a writing folder. Additional information would be compiled using the competencies checklists. Draft books were individual composition notebooks children would maintain throughout the school year. These drafts would be the focus of teacher-student conferences that addressed the next teaching point for that particular child. A copy of the writing, spelling, and handwriting competencies was attached to the back cover for easy reference. As skills were successfully demonstrated over time, I would highlight, re-evaluate, and document every two weeks on each child's permanent file. As the pages were used consecutively and stamped each day with the proper date, the draft books provided an excellent resource for children and their families to observe growth over time.

From the draft books, the children published their edited works. They would have the option of printing or typing their own words or requesting assistance from someone else. I was concerned with the writing *process* (the drafting, the editing conference, and the mini-lesson) more than the writing *product* (the published work). These published works were compiled in a student folder and formed a collection of reading texts for my emergent readers. At the end of the first quarter, most students had progressed from writings that were exclusively drawings with either a single, developmentally spelled word or a sentence consisting of the initial sound of each word. By the end of the second quarter, most children had progressed to copying needed words from a variety of sources (posters, books, other children's published works, etc.) to create correct, complete sentences. By the end of the third quarter, many children had developed the confidence to spell developmentally and then use a variety of sources to confirm or correct their spellings. At the end of the school year, a smaller percentage of children had attempted to write multiple sentences with a variety of punctuation. Some had even attempted stories with conversations.

Major Issues

One of the impressive characteristics of the New Zealand classrooms that I wanted to use with my kindergartners was the high level of student accountability and responsibility for their own learning. In New Zealand, the average class size in new entrants' (five year olds) classrooms was 30 to 35 children and one teacher. Most teachers in this country would have cringed at such child-to-adult ratios. New Zealand teachers found the numbers manageable and the learning successful, because the expectations were clear, high, and achievable. Personal accountability and responsibility were paramount for all students. The children were expected to read at reading times, write at writing times, and help monitor their own learning. It was their responsibility to ask questions to clarify unknown words or concepts. Disrupters were not allowed to control the classroom. The expectation was for learning. There was little tolerance for students who prevented teachers from teaching or other students from learning. The other dynamic that made the high behavioral expectations achievable was that parents shared these expectations and supported the schools' positions.

It had been my experience in past years that discipline issues were the most critical obstacles to teaching, learning, and participating in a variety of activities. If children were unable to observe quietly, were unable to keep their hands and feet to themselves, or demonstrated self-control only when the teacher was watching, the range of possible activities from science experiments to field trips was extremely limited. Therefore, creating a set of competencies for social behaviors would help assess student weakness and plan for instructional support to deal with behavioral issues. Children, parents, and school personnel would need specific behavioral competencies that would improve self-control and theoretically enhance learning opportunities for our classroom.

The following competencies were emphasized, as well as the "grading scale" used for reporting to parents and planning for additional instruction in behavioral skills. Children were expected to attend to stories with or without pictures. Another competency closely aligned to this was participating as listeners and speakers in class discussions. For them to accomplish these successfully, children needed to identify the purpose for participating in the read-alouds or discussions. Therefore, the activities needed to be authentic. Another competency critical to personal accountability and self-monitoring was identifying and requesting clarification of unfamiliar words, phrases, or concepts. This was especially important with regard to clarification and understanding of classroom rules and behavioral expectations. If students were uncertain exactly what it meant to be respectful of school property, they could hardly be expected to meet that expectation. Since I was unable to see what their brains were thinking, I encouraged them in their responsibility for informing me. Another major competency we stressed was completing projects on time with a minimal amount of adult interference. If children were not completing their work because of confusion, it became a personal responsibility to ask for clarification. If another child was distracting them, they had the option to inform the distracter, move to another location, or ask for adult assistance (only as a last resort). If a child was the distracter, he or she would be assigned to another classroom so we could reassess his or her behavior. The expectation was then clear: we come to school to learn.

Once children and parents understood exactly what was expected and why these expectations were reasonable, achievable, and necessary, the opportunities for learning multiplied because the children were able to observe quietly, listen for directions, and ask insightful questions. Science became active, rather than passive, because children practiced self-control and personal accountability. Parent programs increased as children used the opportunity to display appropriate "manners for company" rather than "getting away with something" when guests attracted the teacher's attention. Children not only practiced the expected behaviors, but they also experienced the advantages of being part of a well-behaved classroom. High school students agreed to work with children who could be trusted to behave. Tribal elders visited our classroom to share their culture and traditions with the children, who sat quietly and acted in a respectful manner. Children were trusted with computer equipment, microscopes, and musical instruments. Once the expectations were identified, defined, and applied consistently, there was no need to test (in the traditional sense) for mastery. Could this be applied to other competencies in language arts, science, and mathematics?

I saw these enhanced competency checklists as an opportunity to individualize instruction, assess and evaluate achievement, and plan the next logical learning step. I wanted to avoid grouping children in the traditional static learning groups. My purpose was not to create stigmatizing groups of "robins," "eagles," and "buzzards." What I was looking for within the competencies were small groups of children who might, as an example, benefit from a mini-lesson on a single concept of the writing process. I could pull that group together, present a single concept in a few minutes, and allow them independent writing time to incorporate it into their daily writing. Another group could benefit from a quick read-through emphasizing a reading concept. I would select a book that met that instructional purpose, pull that group together for a brief guided reading, and allow them independent reading time to practice that particular skill. In this way, groups were constantly being formed and reformed without the labeling of high, middle, and low achievers. Success was planned for all students.

Concerned that our competency standards would be reduced to standardized test scores to evaluate student achievement and measure accountability for teachers and students, I was determined to create assessment tools and reporting procedures to inform students, parents, and administrators, and to provide direction for my instructional practices. If the philosophy of Goals 2000 was to offer an alternative to national control or a national curriculum, the philosophy should apply equally well to testing procedures (National Educational Goals Panel, 1994). If a set of standards that improved instruction for all students could be created locally, then why couldn't an assessment procedure to evaluate the effectiveness of those standards be created at a local level? The challenge was to develop an assessment procedure that was valid, authentic, longitudinal, reliable, and objective.

The kindergarten report card previously used provided vague and superficial information (i.e., children can tie shoes, name colors, count to 10). Many children mastered these skills in the first quarter, and the traditional report cards did not allow for the documentation of additional academic growth. This was one of the concerns addressed at a parent meeting. If the standards we had compiled were important, they should be reflected in student reports and evaluations. With the aid of computer technology and input from parents, as well as the approval of my administrators, I developed a database of individual student competencies and achievement. Would this database meet the criterion of creating an evaluation procedure that was valid, authentic, longitudinal, reliable, and objective? If an assessment tool was valid, it would measure what it claimed it would measure. If I documented the reading, writing, and math competencies children consistently demonstrated, I would have a measure of what students had mastered and what the next logical learning step should be (Eichelberger, 1989).

If instructional activities are authentic, they should transfer from the classroom to the real world. In the real world I read words in context. I have never been asked to read a list of unrelated words. In the real world I read a book, discuss it, either condemn it or recommend it, but never do I sit and answer questions at the end of the book! If I were to document children reading words in context, I would have a real-life activity, not an artificial, "only exists in school" activity. Gathering information in a relaxed environment also eliminates the isolating, silent atmosphere that is required for standardized testing (Eichelberger, 1989; Meek, 1993).

If an assessment tracks student learning over an extended period of time, it is longitudinal. Monitoring student progress over time allows for children to have "bad days." Long-term evaluation of student achievement would demand multiple evidences of mastery. A monitoring notebook with running records and competency checklists, draft books, and portfolios would meet this requirement (Eichelberger, 1989).

If an assessment were reliable, participants would consistently score the same if they took the test more than once. I knew that standardized tests all had measurement errors, and that a person's SAT could vary as much as 65 points from one evaluation to the next (Harmon, 1989). If original reading and writing, and verbalization of math, science, and social studies competencies were not consistent over time, then mastery would not have been achieved. My documentation was to be accomplished through multiple demonstrations over extended periods of time, thus meeting reliability criteria (Eichelberger, 1989).

If instruction and assessment incorporated the learning styles, cultures, and backgrounds of individual students and were free from cultural bias, then they were truly objective. Authentic student work would incorporate cultural background, would be open-ended, and would allow for a variety of demonstrations through multiple intelligences (Armstrong, 1994).

If an assessment tool had benefited students, their situation should have improved. Categorizing children on a bell curve or comparing reservation students with students in Boston, or honoring them with permanent membership in remediation programs would not benefit education or self-esteem. Such actions could evoke feelings of defensiveness or guilt in parents. Assessment should allow for more focused instruction and should indicate strengths on which to build and to address weaknesses. Since the criteria to be assessed and evaluated were to be shared with parents and students before entry into kindergarten, this assessment would be honest and open.

Our class piloted those assessment and evaluation tools the entire school year with the intention of re-evaluating prior to the following school year. The goal was not a perfect assessment procedure, but one that addressed the real instructional needs of children, not the statistical needs of educational reformers.

State and National Standards

The reservation community is no longer isolated from the rest of the world. The children of the reservation not only need the skills to contribute to their tribal community, but they also need to master the skills to compete in a global society. If my goal was to meet their educational needs, simply defining and implementing district standards would not be enough. I felt compelled to ensure that the national standards as well as the Nebraska state standards were being addressed. My initial investigation involved the correlation between district and national standards in the area of social studies. The national social studies standards were compiled by agencies such as the National Council of Social Studies (NCSS) and experts in the social sciences. Their suggested standards addressed the inclusion of history, geography, civics, economics, sociology, and anthropology as early as the kindergarten level. Within this broad curriculum there was a flexibility that allowed for a variety of curriculum approaches. The inclusion of all areas of the social science disciplines allowed for a spiraling curriculum that blended with those of our district. Perhaps the most impressive aspect of the national history standards was the emphasis on *understandings*, rather than the memorization of dates and places. The inclusion of literary genres throughout all areas of the curriculum allowed for a truly integrated approach to content presentation. Competencies were classified not by specific grade level, but rather by the broader category of early elementary (K-4). The expectation was for mastery between kindergarten and fourth grade. This correlated perfectly with our classroom philosophy that "not all our flowers bloom at the same time." Specific educational outcomes were based on reflective decision making at our state and district levels.

The Nebraska state standards were similar in construction to the national standards. They were based on the work of professional agencies and individuals in the fields of math, science, social sciences, language arts, and physical education. The Nebraska standards also promoted a spiraling curriculum that allowed for a variety of approaches and instructional methods and materials. State standards effectively bridged the district and national standards by defining mastery, not by assigning competencies to specific grade levels, but by providing a kindergarten through first-grade range of mastery expectancies. In the social studies content area, Nebraska defined ten instructional themes. A single theme could integrate several social studies disciplines, as well as include mathematics, science, and language arts.

The national, state, and local language arts standards for handwriting also reflected this compatibility as demonstrated in Figure 3.3. According to the National Education Goals Panel Guide to Goals and Standards, the goals were designed to be less definitive to allow parents, teachers, and community leaders the latitude to determine what specifically should define education in their districts (National Education Goals Panel, 1994).

Nebraska state standards included an extensive array of suggested parent activities to supplement the content areas. These suggested activities were easily implemented, practical, and closely aligned with school activities. They addressed higher-order thinking skills, as well as knowledge acquisition (State Board of Education, 1998). Collectively, the national, state, and district standards complemented each other. Standards at all levels challenged students, allowed for individualization of instruction, and encouraged a variety of educational methods and materials.

FIGURE 3.3
Comparison of National, State, and Local Standards

NATIONAL STANDARDS (LANGUAGE ARTS)
3. Uses grammatical and mechanical conventions in written compositions

NEBRASKA STANDARDS (CONTENT STANDARDS)
6. By the end of first grade, students will print neatly and correctly
Student demonstrations:

   6.1 Print using appropriate starting points and strokes.
   6.2 Print using a left to right, top to bottom progression.
   6.3 Print uppercase and lowercase letters with recognizable accuracy and comfort.

WINNEBAGO STANDARDS (BENCHMARKS)
At a Pre-writing Level, children will be provided the opportunity to:
   lak.1 create original drawings (representational)

At an Emergent Level, children will be provided the opportunity to:
   lak.2 practice proper grip and posture when writing
   lak.3 print recognizable letters/numerals with proper formation

At an Early Level, children will be provided the opportunity to:
   lak.4 practice correct starting points
   lak.5 apply correct letter/numeral formation in authentic writing activities

At a Fluent Level, children will be provided the opportunity to:
   lak.6 print all upper case letters with proper strokes
   lak.7 print all lower case letters with proper strokes
   lak.8 practice proper letter/word spacing
   lak.9 practice proper letter/numeral alignment
   lak.10 maintain regular letter/numeral size
   lak.11 maintain appropriate pressure
   lak.12 write on lined paper (3 lined primer type)
   lak.13 maintain a legible style with speed

Computerized Record Keeping and Reporting

During this time, report formats arrived at the computer age in our school district. A computerized system instantly compiled group or individual reports, manipulated records for statistical purposes, and accessed information for the tribal court to coordinate intervention strategies for youth in crisis. Attendance was part of the system, and parents and the tribal court were automatically notified of habitual unexcused absences. This computerization presented the challenge of converting information from competency checklists into percentage scores. These percentages were then translated into a letter grade for traditional report cards and cumulative files. A more detailed accounting of each subject and specific competencies, however, could be printed for parents upon request. With all teachers using the same checklist of competencies and the same scoring systems, the exchange of information was more consistent, accessible, and transferable.

Our district had revised our curriculum and developed competencies that reflected both the national and state standards. Parents were informed and pleased with the reporting instruments developed at the kindergarten level. Kindergarten children were learning to be responsible for their own learning. What was now lacking was evaluation of instructional standards for me, the teacher. I have always believed that successful education could occur in a barn, in the absence of expensive, teacher-proof manuals and elaborate computer equipment. I have always believed that successful education requires a competent teacher who: 1) understood children and the acquisition of learning, 2) knew the methods and materials to motivate that learning, 3) continually monitored the progress or the lack of progress in that learning, and 4) accepted responsibility when learning did not occur. I have always viewed the standards for education as incomplete without accountability standards for teachers.

The issue of standards implied some measures of accountability. Students were required to demonstrate mastery of the competencies. If they failed, who would be held accountable? Would the standards be held accountable for expecting too much? Would schools and teachers be held accountable for not meeting instructional needs of students? Would the parents be held accountable for being nonsupportive or neglectful? Would the student be held accountable for being lazy or lacking in ability? Children have been classified as "learning disabled" or "ADHD" when, in my opinion, they have been instructionally disabled. Instructional disabilities occur when children are expected to overcome the challenges of formal academics.

Personal Observations

As an American, I plead guilty to our well-deserved reputation for looking to science and technology to solve a multitude of problems. Americans tend to look for a quick fix for everything from acne to atomic energy concerns. We tend to equate dollars with solutions. My philosophical perspective is that children cannot be assembly-line educated. In an attempt to force education to mass-produce learners, we have herded children into schools in much the same manner that we herd cattle into stock pens. Children are individuals, and as such, have individual needs, experiences, and perspectives. Children will not thrive in a one-design-fits-all environment simply because it is convenient for adults. Kindergarten is a garden of children, not a herd of cattle.

Educational standards, as I was able to implement them in my classroom, have challenged me: 1) to reflect on realistic, yet high expectations for my students, 2) to evaluate and justify my classroom practice, 3) to address individual student needs, interests, and aptitudes, and 4) to document personal accountability with regard to student achievement. The educational standards I helped draft, as well as the national and state standards I have incorporated into the classroom, have improved my teaching and my students' learning. They have forced me to address not only educational competencies, but accountability systems, parental involvement, and documentation procedures. These standards have afforded me logical educational expectations that are high, achievable, and transferable to real life. At the kindergarten level, our district standards have formed the beginnings of a spiraling curriculum that has built-in challenges. Writing local standards has been an experience that required reflection on current teaching practices and reporting procedures.

The district implementation of educational standards formed a cycle of assessment, evaluation, reflection, instruction, and cognition. Once the community evaluation was complete and the competencies defined, the implementation cycle began. *Assessment* and *evaluation* had defined the district needs. *Reflection* upon student needs, interests, strengths, and weaknesses would determine the appropriate approach to *instruction*. With any experience, there is cognition. It is not necessarily the learning the teacher intended. Therefore, assessment of student *cognition* and teacher *evaluation* of that *assessment* must be ongoing. If instruction is to be monitored, this process must be recurring.

References

Armstrong, T. 1994. *Multiple intelligences in the classroom.* Alexandria, Va.: Association for Supervision and Curriculum Development.

Chambers, D. L. 1993. Standardized testing impeded reform. *Educational Leadership,* 50 (5): 80.

Clay, M. M. 1995a. *An observation survey of early literacy achievement.* Hong Kong: Heinemann.

Clay, M. M. 1995b. *Reading recovery: a guidebook for teachers in training.* Hong Kong: Heinemann.

Daniels, H. (Ed.). 1996. *An introduction to Vygotsky.* London: Routledge.

Eichelberger, R. T. 1989. *Disciplined inquiry: understanding and doing educational research.* White Plains, N.Y.: Longman.

Harmon. S. 1989. The tests: trivial or toxic? *Teachers Networking: The Whole Language Newsletter,* 9 (1): 4-7.

Meek, A. 1993. On setting the highest standards: a conversation with Ralph Tyler. *Educational Leadership,* 50 (6): 83-86.

National Education Goals Panel. 1994. *Guide to goals and standards* [Online]. (http://www.negp.gov)

State Board of Education. 1998. *Nebraska reading/writing standards* [Online]. (http://www.nde.state.ne.us/IPS/Issu/AcadStand.html)

4

EDUCATIONAL REFORM IN TEXAS
by Kathy M. Hogan

At the same time that the 1983 publication of *A Nation at Risk* generated nationwide concern that the academic performance and the potential competitiveness of U. S. students in the workforce lagged significantly behind that of students in other countries, the state of Texas began its own educational reform efforts. H. Ross Perot captured the public's attention with his high-profile hearings and proposals, and "no pass, no play" legislation became the symbol of tougher standards. The decade of the '80s was just the beginning of an all-encompassing examination, legislative consideration, and renewal of public education in the state of Texas. Wide-ranging changes were focused on improvements in identifying and meeting student needs, upgrading the quality of instruction, and creating an elaborate accountability system. In two short decades increasing standards and expectations for students, teachers, and school districts have dramatically revamped the Texas public education system.

The Tests

Many of the most significant reforms of the '80s were enacted through House Bill 72 (1984). Class size was limited in grades K-4 to 22, prekindergarten programs for the disadvantaged were established, passing grades were raised from 60 to 70, parents were notified of failing grades every three weeks, and unexcused absences were limited to five per year. Among many other reforms of the decade came the beginning of standardized tests. The Texas Assessment of Basic Skills (TABS), a statewide testing program in reading, math, and writing administered to grades 3, 5, 7, 9, and 11 was created. After the Education Reform Act of 1984, the TABS test was replaced in 1986 by the more difficult Texas Educational Assessment of Minimum Skills (TEAMS), which was developed to parallel the essential elements and curriculum actually being taught in public schools. TEAMS was then replaced in 1990 by the Texas Assessment of Academic Skills (TAAS), a more rigorous test focusing on higher-order thinking skills and problem solving, rather than the basic or minimum skills. Passage of an exit-level TAAS became a graduation requirement. In the early days of standardized testing teachers were petrified by the aura of mystery and ambiguity surrounding the "sealed" tests. They also felt they were testing students on skills they had not yet been taught. Concern from the public arena, parents as well as teachers, caused the testing program to change again in 1993, making the contents of the test more public, moving the fall TAAS test to the spring, and changing the test takers from students in odd-numbered grades to those in grades 4, 8, and 10. Today, the TAAS testing program has been expanded to grades 3 through

8, and includes additional subject areas—reading, writing, and math. The state legislature also mandated end-of-course examinations in several subjects for students in grades 9 through 12, starting in 1994-95.

What Is the TAAS Test?

Virtually everyone inside the walls of a Texas school, from prekindergartners to high school seniors, is affected by the TAAS test. Joining the bandwagon are others who are also affected: parents, community members, policy makers, school board members, the commissioner of education. Why is a single test the focus of so much attention? Part of the reason stems from the ultimate significance given to it. From the initial search for an objective standard on student achievement, the TAAS has come to mean many things to many people.

The Academic Excellence Indicator System (AEIS), better known as the school's report card, gives an account of the TAAS results, which then becomes available for public scrutiny. Schools are rated as exemplary, recognized, acceptable, or unacceptable, based on the percentage of all students, and of each student group (African American, Hispanic, white, and economically disadvantaged) who pass the reading, writing, and math sections of the TAAS. Figure 4.1 summarizes the requirements for each level of performance.

FIGURE 4.1
School Ratings Criteria

Area	Exemplary %	Recognized %	Acceptable %	Not Acceptable %
Achievement, All Students	90	80	40	Less than 40
Achievement, Special Groups	90	80	40	Less than 40
Drop Out Rate	Less than 17	Less than 35	Less than 63	63 or higher
Attendance	94	94	94	93 or less

The AEIS also sets escalating standards, with an annual 5 percent increase expected; thus, the TAAS standard for an acceptable rating should reach 70 percent by the year 2004. As reported by the *Houston Chronicle*, Governor Bush made this comment about the decision, "As we raise the bar, students and schools will rise to the occasion." Future ratings will also include the TAAS results of tested special education students and of students tested on the reading and math sections of the Spanish TAAS. The emphasis placed on the TAAS test ranges from the test driving the curriculum to the test constituting the curriculum. Some might ask, "How can I make learning exciting when all I do is monotonous TAAS drill?" "I don't want to teach to a test," others might say. To alleviate this frustration and address important concerns teachers may have about the TAAS test, several factors must be considered.

First, it is important for teachers to understand that the TAAS test is a criterion-referenced test, not a norm-referenced test. In a criterion-referenced test performance is measured against some prespecified criteria or in relation to a stated standard. Rather than group or norm comparisons, the focus is on specific skills. Second, if the test is based on mastery of standards, then the standards must be specifically stated. To that end Texas has developed the Texas Essential Knowledge and Skills (TEKS) that outlines what children are expected to know and be able to do at each grade level. Third, curriculum alignment with the standards is essential. If the curriculum is aligned with the standards, then what goes into the curriculum should be reflected on the teacher's lesson plans and in the textbooks we use. In essence, then, if all steps are taken, a teacher teaches exactly what is tested on the TAAS test, a test of minimum basic skills. And, in teaching to the test, teachers will help children achieve age-appropriate standards. (And we all live happily-ever-after?)

TAAS is well known and understood; there are no surprises. It is regarded as a fair and stable instrument; the same standards have been applied to every campus and district in the state for five years, and there are published plans through 2003. Teachers work very hard to teach students the skills necessary to pass the TAAS test. They join the bandwagon movements in their own schools to raise test scores, and when they do, everyone celebrates. But, is it right to narrowly define accountability as a test score with only teachers held accountable? The fact that Texas is the first state to directly link teacher evaluations to student test scores on the new Professional Development and Appraisal System (PDAS) has caused statewide concern.

If you ask any of the brightest and best future teachers about to embark upon their teaching careers why they are entering the teaching profession, they will probably tell you that they want "to make a difference in the life of a child." Some might tell you that they have always known that they wanted to be a teacher, ever since a certain teacher made a difference for them, made them feel special, or encouraged them to do their best. Perhaps that critical turning point in their lives occurred later, when another professional career left them feeling unfulfilled. In either case, they are not likely to tell you that they have always aspired to be part of a political or bureaucratic movement to raise TAAS test scores. In their need to be accountable to the bureaucracy, however, they often have to ignore their more deeply felt accountability to meet the needs of individual children.

If the primary purpose of testing were to help teachers evaluate and address individual student learning needs, then the testing would provide valuable information. Teachers fear that the public, the media, and policy makers often see a single test score as an absolute indicator of student learning or teacher effectiveness. Teachers consider assessment a central part of the teaching process and believe that student learning should be evaluated in many ways. Valid assessment should be inseparable from instruction. To them, using standardized tests to assess "nonstandard" children does not reflect the impact of a teacher on the life of a child. It may indicate that the child has or has not learned how to take a multiple-choice test, and it may show how well TAAS objectives were taught and learned at a certain grade level. And teachers believe that many programs that brought great rewards to students, their teachers, and their schools may take a back seat to TAAS-related activities. They believe that the TAAS should be only one component of an assessment plan.

Unfortunately, Texas teachers and students do not all "live happily ever after" just yet. From both sides of the educational spectrum, extremists attempt to politicize educational reform and push their own agendas. Additionally, the uninformed sideliners criticize and condemn the "failure of public schools" to make any worthwhile systemic changes. Apathy creeps into the teaching profession as a defense against the bombardment of another "WHAT NOW?!" Criticism, constant change, and lack of time to effect meaningful changes immobilize many in the face of reform efforts.

Although the TAAS and TEKS do not assess early childhood education, many educators at this level believe that tests can be invaluable tools for the assessment of learning styles, an indicator of a child's strengths and learning needs, and a guide for placement in an appropriate learning environment.

How a child performs on a test on a given day, no matter how powerful the test may be, can only provide a snapshot of the child's potential. The true compass of a child's ability must be considered by viewing a variety of assessment measures gathered over a period of time. The Pre-Kindergarten/Preschool Program for Children with Disabilities (PPCD) focuses on the stages of child development, providing early intervention services which enrich the intellectual, emotional, social, and physical growth of our children. We use a continuum of learning/developmental stages, that recognizes that systematic growth and development occurs continuously over time, at many rates, and in response to many factors. The continuum allows educators to recognize a child's developmental position and plan accordingly: thematic units, centers, selection of materials, assessment strategies, and parent conferences.

The Standards

National educational efforts were gaining momentum to meet the challenges of the 21st century prompted by the 1989 Charlottesville Summit and the creation of the National Education Goals. Texas stakeholders determined that educational reform must raise academic standards, measure student and school performance against those standards, provide schools and educators with the tools, skills, and resources needed to prepare students to reach the standards, and hold schools responsible for the results. A few months after the passage of Goals 2000: Educate America Act, Texas launched Academics 2000 in November, 1994. A state panel developed a State Education Improvement Plan. The panel reviewed the progress of measures and time lines in the plan, and recommended revisions in state education legislation. The state board of education and the U.S. Secretary of Education approved the plan in 1995.

Because of its comprehensive school improvement plan, Texas became the fifth of only six states to be named to the Goals 2000 Education Flexibility Partnership Demonstration Program (Ed-Flex) in 1996. By granting Texas Ed-Flex status, the U. S. Secretary of Education gave the Texas commissioner of education the authority to exempt individual school districts or the entire state from several key federal education laws and regulations that get in the way of community efforts to improve teaching and learning.

The Texas Education Code provides for a foundation curriculum composed of language arts, mathematics, science, social studies, and an enrichment curriculum that includes languages other than English, health, physical education, fine arts, economics, career and technology education, and technology applications. The state board of education identifies the essential knowledge and skills for all courses in the foundation and enrichment curriculum. School districts must adhere to the statewide standards for the foundation curriculum, but may use those for the enrichment curriculum as guidelines to tailor their own programs.

In June 1995, a process known as the Clarification of the Essential Knowledge and Skills began. It is part of the regular review by the state board of education called for in the Texas Administrative Code. Clarification teams were established in each academic area. Rigorous content and student performance standards were evaluated and revised, making them more relevant to the knowledge and skills students will need to be successful in the 21st century. Also in 1995, two Centers for Educator Training were established to train educators in the content and student performance standards. Technology training centers, focusing on the best uses of technology in standards-based instruction, were also established in 1995, as part of the plan for greater integration of technology in curriculum and instruction, a product of the update of the Long-Range Plan for Technology.

Public hearings were held in 1996 to review the proposed Texas Essential Knowledge and Skills (TEKS). The Texas Education Agency (TEA) launched a major public information campaign about the review of the TEKS to ensure maximum public input, including town meetings at the Education Service Centers with a 20-minute introductory video, public service announcements for television, and news releases. A copy of TEKS and comment forms were placed on TENET and on the World Wide Web. Teams of teachers, curriculum specialists, university faculty, parents, and others developed each of the subject-area TEKS with the purpose of ensuring that all students can demonstrate the knowledge and skills necessary to read, write, compute, problem solve, think critically, apply technology, and communicate across all subject areas. A connections team ensured consistent levels of rigor, logical sequence of skill and knowledge development across grade levels, existence of real-world applications, and other factors throughout TEKS.

Rancorous debate at the state board of education meetings prevailed during the entire process prior to approval of the TEKS as the new state-mandated curriculum in July 1997. Members of the board who had been part of the three-year process to develop the TEKS were infuriated with attempts by ultra-conservatives to amend each of the areas of the TEKS. Controversy about several issues dominated the board meetings, such as preserving the board's control over textbook content. The commissioner of education's concern was with what he termed an unfair media portrayal of TEKS as a liberal document, with a specific concern over the status of the social studies TEKS. Despite the controversy, Texas schools did implement the TEKS, in lieu of the older Essential Elements, as the basis for instruction during the 1998-99 school year.

Whereas the 1984 Essential Elements defined what teachers had to teach, the focus of the TEKS is on what students should know and be able to do, while providing for instructional decision making at the local level. Rather than providing "opportunities to engage in" a variety of activities (as stated in Essential Elements), students are now required to demonstrate evidence of understanding. These clear, measurable descriptions of student expectations serve as domains, objectives, and targets for the TAAS.

With the implementation of the new curriculum came the necessity to link TAAS tests with the TEKS. The process began with committees of educators and TEA staff aligning TEKS student expectations with TAAS instructional targets, ensuring an alignment which reflects the focus and organizational structure of the TAAS. Teachers are now more involved than ever in making good instructional decisions about how to implement the TEKS in classroom teaching. As with any set of state standards, no matter how strong, adapting the information to meet local needs is essential. Involving the community in modifying or rewriting the standards and giving teachers the voice in decisions that affect their students and classrooms are key elements of an effective standards movement.

The Humble School District, for example, opted to use the TEKS as a guideline for creating its own standards. Using the comprehensive guide *Designing Standards-Based Districts, Schools, and Classrooms*, (Marzano and Kendall, 1996), Humble has developed standards for birth through grade 12. Nationally recognized for the outstanding education it offers students, the district's mission statement declares, "Our goal is that each student will meet world-class standards in language arts, mathematics, science, social studies, foreign language, physical education, health and the fine arts. Our students will discover and nurture creative talents and learn to be responsible citizens who are self-disciplined and have skills enabling them to become economically self-sustaining. Our students will aspire to a healthy lifestyle and have positive self-worth."

To accomplish that goal and to communicate those expectations to the community, *Curriculum Standards, Grades K-5*, outlines what most children will know and be able to do in each of the subject areas. The curriculum standards are based on research of current district curriculum expectations, national subject-area standards, state Essential Elements, TEKS and TAAS specifications and objectives. The district seeks to promote a curriculum that is rich and worthwhile for all students and that encourages them to solve problems, to be critical and creative, and to make connections among subject areas whenever possible. The Humble standards are for students in kindergarten through grade 5 in language arts, reading, mathematics, science, social studies, art, music, and physical education. The curriculum guides for grades 2 through 5 suggest student activities for acceleration and remediation, and evaluation requirements.

A comprehensive curriculum is based on standards that are developmentally appropriate. Beginning with kindergarten, TEKS standards provide continuity and breadth of student knowledge and skills that become more comprehensive throughout elementary and secondary education. Even though students are not tested until the third grade, the state board of education recognizes the necessity for carefully constructed standards for earlier grades. Beginning in the early childhood years, students develop the processes and skills to become successful problem solvers, to develop appropriate study skills, and to build a conceptual understanding of language and symbols. The state board of education authorized textbook publishers to design preparation booklets for kindergarten that could initiate this process. These booklets help students develop math vocabulary and listening skills that provide the foundation needed for the first TAAS test in the third grade.

Helping students reach more challenging academic standards has led to significant changes in the ways that teachers manage their time and resources. Many teacher leaders in Texas participate in a dynamic and interactive team of capable, committed, and trustworthy individuals who link their talents for successful students.

Accountability

On March 10, 1985, over 200,000 Texas teachers headed to testing sites, equipped with skills of punctuation and capitalization (to name a few), and of course, with their #2 pencils. Their goal was "to topple TECAT" (Texas Examination of Current Administrators and Teachers)—a goal they achieved.

On the heels of the TECAT were other bad ideas. Many of the early teacher appraisal instruments were judged inadequate. In the early days of the Texas Teacher Appraisal System (TTAS), most teachers seemed to believe that they could receive favorable assessments by trotting out their "dog and pony show." When teachers learned how to follow the "Lesson cycle," (state the objective, extend responses, provide for wait time, encourage reluctant learners, relate the lesson to a child's experiences), they realized that it was time to change the evaluation instrument.

Voila! The 1997-98 school year introduced many school districts to the Professional Development Appraisal System (PDAS) with its ominous Domain Eight, linking teacher appraisal to student test scores. A change in the law, brought about by the passage of Senate Bill 1 by the 1995 Legislature, requires that student performance be a factor in teacher appraisal. In fashioning PDAS, Commissioner Moses interpreted "student performance" to mean standardized test scores and specifically the TAAS. Under PDAS, each individual teacher's appraisal would be linked to the TAAS scores of the entire school.

Local school districts were given the option of adopting the PDAS, modifying the PDAS, modifying the TTAS, or adopting a completely new system. Regardless of the system chosen, linking student performance as an element of teacher appraisal had to be evident. In Humble schools, an integral part of the accountability system is the school district's appraisal system, Teacher Objectives and Proficiency

Review (TOP Review) that is similar to the state's PDAS. In addition to 27 criteria in eight domains, teachers are required to work within their grade level team to develop a more personalized growth plan. The team objective, campus improvement plan objective, and the individual objective are related to mutually defined school-wide expectations. Working as teams offers teachers the opportunity to find answers to problems, acquire new skills and methodologies, share technical knowledge, provide assistance to peers, and meet the challenge of standardized testing.

Essential to the collaborative process is increased teacher commitment to the belief in the potential for positive change. As individual teams work together within the schools, the desire for vertical bridging increases. Positive feedback on student progress affirms team efforts, which in turn energize and facilitate further growth. One product of vertical bridging in the Humble schools is the formation of literacy teams. The early childhood literacy team (kindergarten and first-grade teams, with input for the prekindergarten team) collects data within the first few weeks of school on the literacy development of all children. Particular interest is given to the entering first-grade students who are functioning in the bottom third of their class, since these students will be candidates for Reading Recovery or Title 1 intervention. Teachers continue to receive training provided by the district in Balanced Literacy, just one piece of a much larger puzzle required to meet the district and campus goals of earning an exemplary rating on the AEIS.

Those teachers committed to working in schools with high numbers of at-risk children have been especially concerned. It is feared by many that a mass exodus from low-performing schools will result in magnifying a situation that is already distressing. Even in a school district recognized for its quality environment, a shortage of teachers exists. The situation is serious enough that the plea for more teachers is even announced at high school football games. Additionally, schools are staffed with too many teachers on emergency or alternative certifications. Incentive programs have been suggested as ways to recognize and reward teachers in schools that show significant improvement in their TAAS test scores. On one hand, these incentive programs are discouraging to teachers in schools with a high percentage of students who are at-risk and struggling to reach a recognized rating. On the other hand, exemplary schools, which are currently at a 97 percent passing rate, would have trouble showing "significant improvement." Are these teachers not deserving of a pay increase?

The greatest pressure facing a teacher who strives to raise academic standards in his or her class is limited time. Teachers need time to collect observation data of specific behaviors in different contexts, record conversations, and make notes on skills and strategies the student uses. We teachers also need to collect a variety of evidence of learning in our portfolios through process and product samples.

Teachers do not object to being held accountable for the job they do in the classroom. But they insist that accountability must be shared with administrators, local school boards, businesses, parents, and students.

Sandbox Wisdom

According to Robert Fulghum, most of what we really need to know about how to live, and what to do, and how to be, we learned in kindergarten. The rest of what we learn throughout our lives depends upon the solid foundation of our early childhood years. Early childhood is an adventure of colossal magnitude, taking the young child from the security of home to the uncertainty of the big, wide world. Eventually, that big, wide world will become the global schoolhouse of lifelong learning. From sandbox wisdom, the benchmark of early childhood character development, to the real world expectations of problem solving and creative thinking, the future is fashioned. *Goals 2000: A Progress Report* (U.S. Department of Education, 1996) focuses on the role that early learning plays in children's later school success with its first goal: all children must enter school ready to learn. How is a team of preschool educators in the growing community of Humble, affected by a nationwide movement toward educational reform? What place do a test, a set of standards, and accountability have in a preschool classroom? After all, isn't preschool where you play all day, maybe listen to a story or two, eat your breakfast or lunch, and then go home? Real learning happens later, right?

At Lakeland Elementary School, teachers and administrators have answered these questions by providing a quality early childhood education, one that gives children experiences in authentic exploration and discovery. The curriculum and all related aspects must promote exploration, discovery, and the pro-social behaviors, like sharing and cooperating with others, that will promote harmonious relationships among peers. In order to accomplish the immense challenge of meeting the individual needs of a diverse group of early childhood students, tools that best assess and evaluate a child's progress must also be considered.

To reach their full potential, children must learn to be independent in doing, providing, and deciding for themselves. From a young age a child can be encouraged to develop a love of learning, a positive attitude toward school, and experience independence in all developmental domains. Successful experiences in the personal/social, adaptive, motor, communication, and cognitive domains lead to the development of a positive attitude toward learning, leadership qualities, self-expression, problem solving, decision making, and coping skills. A teacher can affect this process by challenging students through small steps and rewarding their effort. She or he will not pamper or coddle reluctant learners, or try to control them with fear. Instead, she or he encourages them to stand on their own feet and take control of their own lives. Independence is fostered when a child makes choices and learns to consider the consequences of his or her actions. By accepting mistakes as stepping stones in the process of learning, a child is able to learn from all experiences, including risk-taking adventures.

In a district where the vision is a safe, student-centered, and supportive environment, collaboration with all community members (students, parents, district personnel, taxpayers, service groups, religious organizations, governmental units, and businesses) is seen as the professional norm. As the district seeks creative solutions to existing challenges, goals and objectives—the basis for the district's improvement plan—are developed by the district and board of trustees. Educational personnel, parents, and community partners work together in district and campus site-based decision-making teams to brainstorm effective ways to prepare students to meet the challenges of the future in an ever-changing society.

To further involve district personnel as stakeholders in educational reform, individual campuses involve each faculty member in goal-setting, planning, and evaluating clear yearly goals as part of the campus improvement plan. The faculty may develop their own mission and belief statements to be adopted by the campus site-based decision-making committee. These efforts are all directed towards helping students and their schools do well on all the current measures.

Responding to Comprehensive Educational Reform

At the national level the U.S. Department of Education recognizes these challenges. The 1993 Goals 2000 Teacher Forum, the beginning of an annual initiative to shift the focus from teachers as objects of reform to teachers as partners in reform, provided teachers with a voice in educational leadership. Among many other questions, the forum addressed the kind of systemic changes needed to challenge all students to meet higher expectations. Forum teachers recommended an increase in the inclusion of teachers in any decision making that affects their students, adequate time to be professional educators, an overhaul of teacher preparation programs, adequate, equitable, and stable funding, and a reshaping of the educational system to prepare students for a competitive, fast-changing world. Subsequent forums have dealt specifically with many of these issues. Teachers from all over the United States were "adopted" by the Department of Education, which provided a personalized "hotline" for teachers to discuss questions and concerns.

Professional associations, such as the Texas State Teachers Association (TSTA), also recognize these concerns. By participating in the annual TSTA Critical Issues Conference, teachers are kept up to date on hot topics in education and are provided with the tools and resources to deal with them on the local level. The TSTA initiative has provided teachers with several creative suggestions for managing time and restructuring the school day to meet student needs, and keep up with the demands of a changing educational system.

Delta Kappa Gamma, Alpha State, a society for key women educators, also emphasizes our changing educational system in its program goals for the next biennium. Stimulating discussions with other educators as they interface collaboratively with the community increase the power of a teacher's voice in implementing changes. At Lakeland Elementary we are committed to facing these opportunities for growth through dialogue and problem solving. Within our building (and buildings all across this nation, state, and district), are talented teachers who can provide their teammates with excellent ideas and strategies to meet student needs. Peer coaching and mutual mentoring (where one's area of expertise, ideas, and teaching strategies can be shared with another) strengthen individual teachers. Also at the local level, the school district has followed the lead of the state in providing an avenue for involvement in local reform efforts. Community forums and strategic planning committees are two means by which citizen involvement and school cohesiveness can be achieved.

Where morale is high, a clear sense of identity as an effective team member is also present. A cohesive school buzzes with the pervasive atmosphere of important business. There is a unified effort to support the school's goals, and there is celebration when those goals are met. The power and potential of school reform lie with innovative and caring teachers. Samuel Johnson wrote, "What we hope ever to do with ease, we must learn first to do with diligence." With diligence we seek a higher standard; with diligence we will align the pieces of the standards puzzle. With heart we will make a difference in the life of a child; with pleasure we will celebrate!

Last year, after the TAAS test, a fourth-grade student at Lakeland walked up to her teacher. "I didn't make my goal," she said, waiting for a response from her teacher. Before her teacher could muster the right words of comfort and encouragement, the child's face beamed with delight. "I didn't make my goal," she repeated. "I beat it!"

When so many teachers from prekindergarten days through TAAS test days work to teach a child to take responsibility for his or her own learning, and that child "beats" his or her own goal, the whole school celebrates. It may not show up on a chart presented at a school board meeting, and it may not be reflected in an improved rating on the Academic Excellence Indicator of the school's report card. But one child reaffirms the value of the whole process. The hard work is all worthwhile: the needs assessments, the instructional interventions, the grouping arrangements, the re-teaching and the evaluating. All of the daily struggles are wrapped up in one small victory, giving teachers the impetus to meet the next challenge. It seems that change almost always arrives at our doorstep wrapped up in thick brick walls. While the focus of most initial discussions on change is on the barriers, administrators and teachers must get beyond these barriers to the place where professional conversations can be focused on the bottom line—higher student achievement.

Administrators have been known to do eccentric stunts in response to raised TAAS scores. Seeing a principal kiss a pig or sing from the rooftop of the school building may be motivating and humorous. Long-range systemic change, however, stems from much more thoughtful deliberations on student learning. The first step, then, is to provide teachers with the time and space within the school day to dialogue about their beliefs. Linking beliefs with classroom practices can be the focus of brainstorming sessions. Many seemingly insurmountable issues faced by teachers can be solved in brainstorming sessions. It is the role of administrators, then, to be creative and flexible in scheduling collaboration time within the school day.

Teachers must be dedicated to understanding the learning processes going on in their classrooms. New research involving the brain will give teachers important information on what a child does when he or she engages in learning, and how he or she interacts with new experiences in his or her environment. Teachers also need to be focused on what a child can do, not what he or she struggles to do. It is essential that learning be built on what a child has control of in his or her environment. By focusing on a child's strengths, he or she will be more motivated to learn. Learning will seem easier and more fun.

We have struggled with the standards, felt pressure from standardized tests, evaluation instruments, and the critics of the public education system. The truth of the matter is that there is no comparison between the quality of teaching that takes place today and the teaching of the early '80s. Before the standards movement, we teachers just scratched the surface. Now we access, diagnose, evaluate, and then teach. We don't just teach, but we know how, why, and when to teach. We are making more connections, using more tricks and applications, rather than teaching isolated skills. Teachers are excited about the challenge of the investigations, then building learning on an individual basis.

The standards movement is alive and well in the state of Texas. One final question remains. Will there be dedicated and qualified teachers in tomorrow's classrooms, or will the exodus from the teaching profession continue? Until the policy makers realize the significance of the role that teachers play in building the future, the lack of planning time, their inadequate salaries, and their powerlessness will cause even dedicated teachers to leave the profession. A caring teacher with a dream that he or she can make a difference is the most important ingredient in educational reform. All of the tests, standards, and accountability systems mean nothing if they are not implemented by competent, qualified teachers. Texas children are counting on them to be there and depending on them to lead the way.

References

Marzano, R. J., and J. S. Kendall. 1996. *Designing Standards-Based Districts, Schools, and Classrooms.* Alexandria, Va.: Association for Supervision and Curriculum Development.

U.S. Department of Education. 1996. Goals 2000, *A Progress Report.* Washington, D.C.: Author.

5 CALIFORNIA, THE GOLDEN STATE

by Carol Jago

Many educators worry that in California's rush to raise academic standards the state will end up penalizing those children who, through no fault of their own, have not been adequately prepared to meet these standards. Maybe we need to rethink our concept of a "standard."

The Rush to Standards

The traditional mental image of a standard is one of a crossbar, a barrier that students must break through if they are to be deemed proficient, a finish line of sorts. But the first definition of the noun "standard" in the Oxford English Dictionary is "a flag, sculptured figure, or other conspicuous object raised on a pole to indicate the rallying point of an army; the distinctive ensign of a king, commander, nation or city." Replacing the traditional image with this one might help to make the trend toward academic standards a rallying point. When children are not making the progress we expect, resources would be marshaled to make sure that they do.

It is not until the tenth entry for "standard" in the Oxford English Dictionary that a reader comes to "an authoritative or recognized exemplar of correctness, perfection or some definite degree of quality." Identifying exemplars in education is easy; the difficult part is making sure all students have what they need to be able to achieve them.

California currently has in place content standards adopted by the state board of education for language arts, mathematics, science, and history/social science. (See California Department of Education, 1998, for all California standards documents). A Commission for the Establishment of Academic Content and Performance Standards was formed in 1996 and charged by the California legislature to develop grade-level, world-class standards in these four subject areas. According to the commission, the documents "reflect guidance and input from countless members of the California teaching community, parents, administrators, and business leaders helped define key issues." These standards are meant to serve as the basis of a statewide assessment.

The documents are wonderful. Anyone in his or her right mind would want children in California to know and be able to do the things the standards describe. In an ideal world, they could provide a model rallying point. The problem is achieving these standards in substandard conditions. Compared with other states, California is at the bottom in terms of per pupil spending and at the top in terms of English language learners and children living in poverty. Thirty percent of our kindergartners come to school speaking no English. With burgeoning enrollment,

California is going to need 300,000 new teachers by the year 2005. In 1998, the state was forced to grant 21,000 emergency credentials in order to staff classrooms. School buildings are in abysmal physical condition; yet even in a year of budget surplus, legislators cannot agree on a bond issue for funding repairs and new construction. For a "golden" state, California's schools are more than a bit tarnished.

The other problem we struggle with is assessment. In the interim between the development of standards and the development of matching test items, California has administered Harcourt Brace's Stanford 9 tests in grades 2 through 11. To no one's surprise, our students performed below the national average in every subject area in almost every grade. (Seventh- and eighth-grade reading scores were at the 52nd and 53rd percentile.) Urban districts such as the Los Angeles Unified School District reported reading and math scores in the 23rd percentile. Rather than rallying teachers and students to work harder, such results feed discouragement.

I cannot blame Governor Pete Wilson and the state board of education for wanting to measure the quality of education in California. They have a right to know. But what made no sense was that in many areas of the Stanford 9 test, particularly in science and history, the test items bore no relation to what students were being taught in school. For example, at my high school about a third of the ninth-grade class is enrolled in physical science, another third in a technology/science course, and the rest in biology. If a state test is going to ask all ninth-grade students to answer the same set of science questions and then compare students on the basis of their answers, all students should be taught the same material.

The California Science Content Standards were written to "raise the level of expectation for what students know and are able to do at each grade level by defining the essential skills and knowledge in science that will enable our students to compete with their peers from around the world." It is a laudable goal. But before that can happen, California will need much closer correspondence between what is taught and what is tested.

Accountability or Fool's Gold?

A supermodel was recently reported to have remarked, "It was God who made me so beautiful. If I weren't, then I'd be a teacher." Now I have never strolled down a runway and so may be quite mistaken, but it seems to me that teaching requires a great deal more divine intervention than posing does. Some days imparting even one thing to one child feels like a minor miracle.

That is why I find plans that would base teacher evaluations on students' test scores so troubling. Teachers should most definitely be held accountable for student performance, but there is no simple formula for equating teaching with learning. All I have to do is compare two of my own classes to illustrate the problem.

In my honors class, all but three or four students have made significant gains since September. These teenagers have read eight books, written six essays, and taken part in daily class discussions about literature. As a result, I can demonstrate with papers from their portfolios that their writing has improved dramatically. Though we have no comparative test scores for these students, I believe their ability to read challenging texts has also increased. They have certainly had plenty of practice.

During this same interval in my regular English class, all but three or four students have made little progress. Those few students who have aren't necessarily smarter than the rest, nor were they privy to a magic formula for pleasing Mrs. Jago. They simply paid attention in class, completed their homework, studied for tests, and read the assigned books. The others did not.

Rating my performance as a teacher on the basis of student growth from the honors class would make me look like a super-teacher. Using the regular class as a measure makes me seem barely adequate. Same teacher, different results. Not all low student test scores are the products of poor instruction.

If teachers are to be held accountable, and I believe they should be, so must others. School principals must be held accountable for providing a safe environment for teaching and learning. They need to find alternatives for disruptive students so that those who want to learn are able to work. They must also keep administrivial distractions to a minimum and consider classroom time sacred.

Students must be held accountable, too. Though many must work in the evening to support their families and have limited time for schoolwork after 3 p.m., too many waste the hours they have. Every day I see students doing anything but what their teacher has asked: flipping through *Bride* magazine, writing notes, chucking sticks of gum across the room, staring off into space. This behavior is rarely seen in an honors class.

I accept responsibility for students who do not engage as I would hope, and continue to try the best I can to find ways to motivate them. Test scores depend on it. What I refuse to do is turn my lessons into games and pretend that learning does not require determined student effort.

I suppose it's possible that supermodels have special insight into how to teach children and that, were they not so beautiful, education would benefit enormously from their contribution. For the time being, however, I would advise the supermodel to keep her day job.

Panning for Gold on the Pacific Rim

Californians go hot and cold on Japanese education. One day we beat our schools up for not producing students who can compete on math tests with their peers across the Pacific. The next day we congratulate ourselves that our teenagers are better balanced, more creative, and less likely to commit suicide. This vacillation produces plenty of noise in the public arena but precious little curricular reform.

In a study of eighth-grade mathematics classrooms in Japan and the United States, James Stigler, a psychology professor at UCLA, discovered that a great deal more than teaching methods was influencing student performance. Take classroom interruptions, for example. While videotaping randomly selected classes in the two countries, Stigler found that 31 percent of the American lessons were interrupted by some kind of intrusion; in Japan this never happened. (See California State University Institute for Education Reform, 1998).

I would have expected that videotaping paraphernalia might have skewed the sample, but this was not the case. Despite the obvious presence of cameras, interruptions still occurred in almost a third of U.S. classrooms. When Japanese educators saw these tapes, they couldn't believe that someone would interrupt a math lesson and distract students, as happened in the U.S. classroom. For them a lesson is a highly valued event—something like a church service—that no one would think of interrupting to look for the custodian or remind students to pick up their I.D. cards at lunch.

Another remarkable finding of Dr. Stigler's concerned homework. Most Americans assume that one of the reasons Japanese students score better than ours on comparison tests is that they do more homework. In fact, researchers found very little emphasis on homework in Japan, particularly by the time children were in eighth grade. Only 24 percent of the Japanese teachers assigned homework compared with over 90 percent of the American teachers. A great deal of math teachers' time focuses specifically on homework management. Instructors check that it has been done, go over the correct answers, assign the next day's pages, and then help students with new work. On Friday they give a quiz.

Japanese instruction looks nothing like this. Highly teacher-directed, the focus is on problem solving, rather than on answering a set of assigned questions. In the U.S., students complete seatwork to practice the procedure being taught. In Japan, teachers ask students to solve a problem that they've never seen before or to use mathematical reasoning to prove something. Teachers pose rich problems that students are expected to struggle with until a solution is found. According to Stigler's study, "Fifty-four percent of the Japanese lessons included proofs. None of the American lessons included proofs."

Something else that might surprise former inhabitants of California math classrooms is the use of the chalkboard. In Japan, the board is considered the record of the entire lesson being taught. Instructors begin at the left side, introduce a problem, examine various solutions and concepts for solving the problem, and end on the far right of the board, rarely erasing previous steps. When asked about this, Japanese teachers explained that they don't expect their students to be paying attention every minute of the lesson (some things don't seem to change from country to country) so they design a lesson structure that allows students to daydream and then refocus with an entire visual record of the lesson in front of them. Part of curriculum planning in Japan involves designing what the chalkboard is going to look like at each stage of the lesson.

One oft-cited solution to California's poor math scores is more teacher training. In fact preservice training for teachers in California, where there is no undergraduate education major but, rather, a required fifth year of graduate study, is actually longer than it is in Japan. The difference is that the average Japanese teacher entering the profession knows more mathematics. Japanese high school graduates are about four years ahead of average California math students. Compounding this discrepancy in content knowledge is the fact that because teaching is a highly desirable career in Japan, math teachers typically come from the top half of their academic classes.

Will higher standards put our children back at the top of the global list? Will new textbooks, more teacher education, longer and louder speeches by the governor? Maybe. But as long as announcements about the pep rally still punctuate instructional time, we should not be surprised that California students fall short. Interruptions send a powerful message to children about what their school and society value most. If this state wants to improve education, they need to stop interrupting me when I am trying to teach.

When So Many Don't Speak English

We used to call them ESL students to indicate that English was their second language. Then it was LEP for Limited English Proficient. The current term of choice is ELL, English Language Learners. But whatever the label, this growing body of students is challenging California educators in innumerable ways. According to recently released data from the department of education, there are currently 1.4 million Limited English Proficient students in our public schools. This is one quarter of the public school enrollment.

To give you some idea of the growth rate of this population, there has been a 141 percent increase since 1985. And almost 42 percent of the statewide total classified as LEP in kindergarten through grade 6 were enrolled in Los Angeles County. The first language of 80 percent of these children is Spanish.

That the primary goal for these children is to learn English is not in question. How to make it happen, however, often is. Bilingual programs, dual immersion programs, transition programs, sheltered programs, and specially designed instruction all have their advocates. Properly executed, any of these methods can work. What doesn't work, and, unfortunately, what all too many children experience in their first six years of school, is a helter-skelter approach to learning English. One year they have a bilingual teacher; the next year their teacher speaks only English. One year their content subjects are taught in their primary language; the next year no Spanish-speaking geometry teacher can be found, and they are learning math in English. One year the language on the playground is Spanish; the next year they have moved to a campus where 60 languages are spoken.

Though student mobility is a separate issue, it is not unrelated to English language instruction. Given that in many of our urban schools up to 30 percent of the student body is new in any school year, what we need in California is a coherent, systematic method for teaching children to speak English. A mandated curriculum? A one-size-fits-all program for children? What about local control? What about our child-centered curriculum and the belief that teachers teach children, not subjects? In answer I can only say that I think the most important thing we can do for all our children is to help them become literate in English. Without this, they will forever play catch-up, both in school and in the job market. What I want for English language learners is exactly the same thing I want for my own child—a fair chance to compete in the marketplace.

When asked if non-native speakers of English will be expected to meet the state content standards, the board of education has replied, "Yes, non-native speakers of English who graduate from high school in California should be able to achieve at the level called for in the standards. It is clear that holding them to other, lesser standards would be a disservice." Helping students whose first language is not English to meet the rigorous, world-class standards is an enormous challenge, particularly when there is so little agreement over methods of instruction.

In 1997, more than 5,800 schools statewide had at least 20 students with limited English skills. Of those schools, 1,150 did not move a single student into English fluency. For more than half of these schools, this was the second year in a row of complete futility. Overall, fewer than 7 percent of limited English students are becoming fluent each year.

While such figures might sound like an indictment of bilingual education, the truth is that many of these schools are teaching their students only in English. It is possible to identify individual schools where bilingual education, English immersion, dual immersion, or sheltered English classes are working, but for the past decade there has been no statewide consensus about what works best. As Douglas E. Mitchell, education professor at the University of California at Riverside, explains, "This is a huge problem. The system is swamped. People have strong beliefs about what should work, but they don't have strong evidence on what does work." (Public Education, 1999, p. 22.)

As a result, in June 1998, frustrated voters passed Proposition 227, the Unz initiative, banishing bilingual education from California classrooms. Imagine an earthquake. The mandate requires that students with limited English be placed in a year-long English immersion program and, in the following year, mainstreamed into regular classes. The impact of this pedagogical about-face is likely to cause aftershocks for years to come.

Choosing a Book By Its Color

The California Commission for the Establishment of Academic Content and Performance Standards debated loud and long about whether to include a list of recommended readings in the document. In the end they did not. Instead the standards state that "Students will read and understand grade-level-appropriate informational materials. They will analyze the organization patterns, arguments, and positions advanced. Students will also read and respond to historically or culturally significant works of literature conducting in-depth analyses of recurrent patterns and themes."

I was delighted to see this emphasis on literature. Influenced by the cry of employers for graduates with workplace literacy, too many standards documents are recommending that students study informational texts, films, and multimedia resources instead of great literature. Now to readers with only painful memories of being dragged through *The Scarlet Letter* and *Great Expectations*, this may appear a welcome shift, but I would like to argue that the study of literature leads to a deep literacy that will transfer to any and every workplace. I also believe that literature works miracles.

The Association of Literary Critics and Scholars warns against standards that designate popular texts as worthy of classroom study. They believe, and I agree, that when illustrations, advertisements, television, and other sources of "graphic and visual messages" are included in the curriculum, too little time is left for literature. If these texts replace more traditional readings, high schools will graduate young people who have never seen Circe turn men into swine, who have never sailed past Scylla and Charybdis, and who have no knowledge of the dangers lurking in the Land of the Lotus Eaters. Scoff if you like, but Odysseus' adventures offer teenage readers a useful map for internal navigation. Without the classics they will be truly at sea.

When the study of literature can accomplish so much—and so much that law enforcement and social services struggle in vain to accomplish—we abandon it at our peril. Authentic literary study needs to retain its place of prominence in high school English.

The wisdom of the commission's decision to avoid publishing a list of required titles in the standards document was demonstrated in San Francisco. Shortly after the release of the language arts standards, two school board members in San Francisco Unified proposed a revision of their district reading list. They recommended a quota system to insure that writers of many ethnicities, as well as gay and lesbian writers, would be included in students' required reading. Though it began as a genuine attempt to revise a list dominated by white male authors, the initiative became a free-for-all of self-interest and a joke in the public eye.

My own district, the Santa Monica Malibu Unified, has not been badgered by critics for the good reason that our students have been reading multicultural titles along with the classics for the past ten years. Unlike their San Franciscan counterparts, Santa Monica High School students are regularly assigned a broad range of quality literature.

The ninth-grade curriculum, for example, includes *Romeo and Juliet* by William Shakespeare, as well as *Like Water for Chocolate* by Laura Esquivel; *Hiroshima* by John Hersey and *Night* by Eli Weisel; *The House on Mango Street* by Sandra Cisneros and *The Bluest Eye* by Toni Morrison; *Farewell to Manzanar* by Jeanne Wakatsuki Houston and *Metamorphosis* by Franz Kafka; *Cool Salsa*, which is a bilingual collection of Latino poetry and *Somehow Tenderness Survives*, which is a short story collection from South Africa. Apart from *Romeo and Juliet*, not every text is read by every student. Teachers have the professional discretion to choose the books they believe will best foster their charges' developing literary sensibilities.

About ten years ago I became interested in the genre of memoir for my tenth-grade students. I chose Maxine Hong Kingston's *Woman Warrior* and Richard Wright's *Black Boy*, not because they filled particular ethnic boxes, but because they were the most powerful texts I could find by writers examining their own childhoods for answers to how and why they had become who they were. In this course I develop the theme of a hero's journey through Homer's *Odyssey* and *Beowulf* and then move on to contemporary stories such as those of Kingston and Wright. Along the way I also attempt to do justice to the monster's side of the story by having students read John Gardner's *Grendel* and Mary Shelley's *Frankenstein*.

Other titles from the tenth-grade curriculum include, of course, *Julius Caesar*, as well as *Lord of the Flies, Catcher in the Rye, Cyrano de Bergerac, The Joy Luck Club, All Quiet on the Western Front,* and *Bless Me, Ultima* by Rudolfo Anaya. Since the glorious Kenneth Branagh version of *Much Ado About Nothing* appeared on video, I have invariably added that Shakespearean comedy to our list.

The biggest problem with the San Francisco School Board reading list was not that it was too white or too male, but that it was too short. I believe it is reasonable to expect students to read 15 to 20 books during the course of a school year and at least three more during the summer. I invariably assign a novel over winter and spring breaks and lose not a moment of sleep over students who tell me they will be otherwise occupied. Taking a plane? That's a perfect time to read. Visiting relatives? Grandma will be proud to see you with a book. Working a job? What better way to relax when you get home than with J.D. Salinger.

When I asked my ninth graders to read the *Los Angeles Times* news story about the San Francisco controversy and write about what they thought, Gabe said: "I think people should read whatever they want to read. If the book is good, who cares what color the author is. I would read any book by anybody." Miguel commented, "I think that they should balance it, putting Latinos, African Americans, Whites, and Chinese on the list. Everybody can be a good writer. For me a writer is not determined by his race but by how well he writes. We have to learn not to be racist because hate doesn't bring anything but destruction." I am very sure that this is exactly the kind of insight that the San Francisco School Board wants its students to have. Mandating quotas, however, is not the best way to inspire it.

Responding to Mandates

Not long after the commotion over book titles was settled with a compromise list of both classical and contemporary multicultural literature, San Francisco Unified found itself once more in the news. This time it involved San Francisco high school administrators mandating that teachers raise last year's grades by 5 percent.

In a memo sent out at Balboa High School by assistant principal Gloria Galindo, teachers were given until June to "increase the number of As, Bs and Cs by 5 percent over last year's grades" (Asimov, 1998). Understandably insulted, many teachers said they would simply ignore the order. Principal Elaine Koury denied that she and assistant principal Galindo wanted teachers to inflate student grades. According to Koury, "This is an opportunity for people to enter into discussion about how they can change their strategies to help more students succeed."

It seems to me that it is the student body, not the faculty, the principal should be addressing. If individual teachers have unfair grading practices, Koury should by all means work with them to change, but to instruct professional teachers to raise their average grades by 5 percent is nonsense. For grades to rise, it is students, not teachers, who need to rethink what they do.

One of the hardest graders I know is Harry Gordon at Huntington Beach High School. He also has the reputation of being one of the best American literature teachers around. His students rarely earn As, but when they do, they know it means something very special. Scrupulously fair, as well as frighteningly well-organized, Mr. Gordon hands out his final exam question to both parents and students at the very beginning of his year-long course. There is nothing hidden about what he expects students to be able to do come June. Instructing teachers like Mr. Gordon to assign higher grades in effect sends them the message—intentional or not—to lower their standards. More students may wind up feeling good about getting decent grades, but we are setting them up for a fall.

Statistics on grade inflation are quite dramatic. In 1996, 33 percent of freshmen at UCLA reported having an A average in high school compared with 28 percent in 1995 and 12.5 percent in 1969. Can students really have gotten this much smarter? Michael Kirst, Stanford education professor and co-director of Policy Analysis for California Education, explains, "If grades are inflated and don't measure the true achievement of the students, they become eligible for universities but cannot succeed academically when they get there."

Pressure on urban high schools to increase University of California eligibility among their students is intense. But genuinely increasing student eligibility will mean forgetting about raising grades and focusing on improved instruction. We need to insure that every student in California has well-prepared, committed teachers like Mr. Gordon, and we need to keep our promise that each child has a proper textbook for every course. Teachers need to demand from their students more, not less, for their A's.

Imagine a high school principal suggesting that the basketball coach lower the hoop by 5 percent so that more students would be able to score. While players might have fun at practice, few would thank that coach or principal at their next away game. I have no doubt administrators at Balboa High School had their students' best interests at heart.

Spinning Straw into Gold

What teachers need to put standards into practice is obvious to any teacher. Unfortunately, it is much less obvious to everyone else. Witness the following conversation described by Barbara Storms:

> We've all been there. As we settle into our seat on a plane or train or other public transportation, tucking our bag under the seat, toy with how to spend the next few hours catching up on papers, catching up on reading, or catching up on sleep, IT happens. The neatly dressed and manicured person, in my case a man, who's just stuffed his matching laptop computer and brief case under the seat in front of him asks, "What do you do?"
>
> Quickly I size him up. Can he be trusted or am I opening myself up for the deluge? I run through my prepared list of conversation stoppers—mortician, belly dancer, IRS tax auditor. He looks relatively harmless; his tone seems innocent. I decide to say it, "I work in public education."
>
> Like a professional baseball pitcher revving up for his best pitch, the passenger's widening eyes indicate his pitch is on the way. He starts in, "When I was in school, nah nah nah." He continues to list all his perceived limitations of the current educational system. Then he blasts, "Teachers get paid too much."
>
> That's it! He's crossed the line. I politely ask through a clinched smile, "And what do you do?" hoping to distract the attack. He

interrupts his barrage long enough to comment, "I'm in computers," then continues, "Teachers...."

Undaunted, I probe. "What do you do with computers?"

"We design customized database platforms for big companies." And still he persists, "And what's happened to discipline....?"

Losing my patience, I interrupt. "What do you do with these platforms? Do you design them? Sell them?" "I interface with companies to ensure that our product meets their needs," he explains.

I think to myself, now it's my turn. "Do you have a computer on your desk at work? You probably use e-mail don't you?" I question.

"Of course. I couldn't do my work without my computer or e-mail," he comments.

"And I assume you have a phone on your desk."

Looking a little surprised, he comments. "Certainly. How could I do business without one?"

I continue with the probe, "Do you have access to a fax and a copier?"

A bit of suspicion begins to creep into his eyes, "Of course."

"And I suppose you have an assistant to take calls, set up meetings, and format your reports?" Cocking his head a bit and squinting to get a better look at me, he mumbles, "Yes."

Raising my voice a bit, I query, "When you interface with these companies are you meeting with only one company at a time or representatives from several companies at once?"

"One at a time" he mumbles without emotion.

"Now imagine this," I gibe, "you don't have an office, a computer, or an assistant. The only phone is down the hall and shared by 15 other customer representatives. There's one fax machine for the entire company and it's in another building. Now imagine that you have to meet with a group of 35 customers from 35 different companies all at the same time. You only get to see them for 50 minutes before they leave and another 35 representatives from 35 different companies come in. You get to repeat this five times a day. In five hours you see about 200 representatives from 200 companies. How effective would you be?"

Smugly, he states, "There's no way that would happen."

I reply in a solid, unemotional voice. "It does happen. Every day in schools across the country, teachers work with large numbers of students, each student with special and specific needs. Teachers do their work without computers, phones, or access to e-mail, faxes, or copiers. Most teachers design and create their own materials without assistants. Teachers are asked to do their work without even the most rudimentary kinds of support that business people take for granted. Try doing what teachers do for just one day and you'll think differently about schools."

By the time I finish, he's found his book and buried his face so only his cheeks and forehead show. I don't think we'll be talking more this trip.

Barbara Storms dramatizes the dilemma classroom teachers face every day. Of course we want our students to achieve world-class standards. But as long as conditions for teaching and learning remain substandard, the likelihood of any standards document ever becoming more than lovely words on a page is remote.

References

Asimov, N. 1998. Teachers told to pump up grades. *San Francisco Chronicle*, April 4.

California State University Institute for Education Reform. 1998. *Lessons in perspective: How culture shapes math instruction in Japan, Germany and the United States.* Sacramento, Calif.: Author.

California Department of Education. 1998. *California language arts: Reading, writing, listening and speaking content standards.* Sacramento, Calif.: Author.

Public education: California's perilous slide. 1999. *Los Angeles Times*, May 18.

DEVELOPING RIGOROUS STANDARDS IN MASSACHUSETTS

by James Kelleher

Education reform in Massachusetts is an ambitious project that sometimes finds itself being sidetracked by political squabbling and scapegoating. This was particularly true in 1998, when newly devised exams were administered to students as well as aspiring teachers, with the lackluster results appearing in the midst of a gubernatorial campaign. Education reform efforts in Massachusetts have been the source of some notoriety. The chairman of the state board of education at that time, John Silber, was outspoken and rather autocratic in his leadership style. And so many prospective teachers failed the test required for certification that education in this state became the butt of jokes and a topic for debate on national talk shows. Education reform is a popular issue for an election year, and rightly so, since lots of money has been spent on improving student achievement through rigorous standards, and people want to see results. But more light, rather than heat, needs to be shed on this debate, because education reform must maintain the same focus well beyond the election year. This chapter seeks to understand how educators are dealing with these efforts, and what we need to make education reform a success for all.

The Context for Reform

The Massachusetts Education Reform Act (MERA) of 1993 was passed with the primary goal of raising standards for students and teachers and reducing funding inequities in the state. It is a sweeping initiative that calls for curriculum frameworks, outlines standards in different subjects, allows charter schools to be created, and provides extra funding to state communities, with the lion's share going to poorer and urban districts. The law increases the instructional time teachers spend with students and also seeks to instill accountability through assessments; thus, prospective teachers and administrators in the Commonwealth must pass an exam, and students in grades 4, 8 and 10 are being tested as well. The stakes are high for everyone: by 2003, students will need to have passed the tenth-grade test in order to graduate. And it seems likely that the testing process will be expanded in the future.

A reform effort of this magnitude requires vigilance and careful oversight to maintain so many high-stakes initiatives effectively; achieving this has been a challenge. While urban districts have seen a boost in their per pupil spending, many suburban districts have complained that skyrocketing student enrollments have eroded their spending power. The law does not account for changes in enrollment growth and construction costs, even though these are significant concerns for many superintendents in the state. Meanwhile, several urban districts have been criticized for misspending education money. The goal of the reform act for poorer cities such as

Brockton, for example, was to raise standards and make the educational experience for students there as rich as it is for students in more affluent suburbs. But, despite a recent audit reflecting a $25 million boost in the school budget, during that time fourth-grade scores on the Massachusetts Educational Assessment Program (MEAP) declined, even though the average scores statewide increased. The MEAP exams have been replaced by the Massachusetts Comprehensive Assessment System (MCAS), a more comprehensive exam first administered in spring 1998. Aside from the troubling low test scores, the audit also revealed that the city was spending reform money to pay for armed school police officers, who wear bulletproof vests and carry semiautomatic pistols during school emergencies. The press has been quick to pick up on inconsistencies such as this. Yet the department of education has at times seemed to be overwhelmed by the scope of education reform, and it has not been consistent in providing districts such as Brockton with the coaching they need to make this reform work.

The arena of state politics has proven to be a considerable distraction from the work of education reform. Politicians have embraced the issue of education reform with fervor, although detractors have noted that this is more election-year grandstanding and political posturing than a reflection of deeply held values. They have threatened to eliminate tenure (or "professional teacher status" as it is now called) because it protects poor teachers, and to subject all teachers to certification exams; they have discussed closing any school where more than 20 percent fail the state test. The speaker of the state House of Representatives even denounced would-be teachers who failed their certification tests as "idiots," although he later retracted this as "impolitic." But how serious are politicians about reform? For example, the bill to require all teachers to pass the certification test was filed toward the end of the legislative session, with little time for it to be debated.

Politicians have countered that they are genuinely concerned about raising standards in Massachusetts, denying that their rhetoric has reduced reform efforts to sound-bites and teacher-bashing. They have supported creating a corps of master teachers to train apprentices, as well as establishing future teacher clubs. The senate president, Thomas Birmingham, has suggested using the state budget surplus to pay generous signing bonuses of $20,000 to attract high-quality new teachers to Massachusetts public schools. While many agree that this type of financial incentive would help draw new teachers to Massachusetts, they point out the need to spread it over several years, to allow teachers to interact with mentors and grow professionally through reflection of their own practice.

Perhaps the most charismatic and controversial person in education reform is the ex-chairman of the state board of education, John Silber. Silber gained recognition as president of Boston University, which he transformed from a nearly bankrupt school to one with national recognition. His leadership style has been described as that of a theory X, top-down manager who does not refrain from speaking his mind. But this often has gotten him into trouble; his outbursts, known as "Silber shockers," were blamed for dooming his 1990 gubernatorial campaign. Nevertheless, his opponent in that race, former Governor William Weld, saw in Silber's unabashed, unrelenting zeal the ability to shake up the cumbersome education bureaucracy. For many years, Silber was Massachusetts' education czar, praised on the one hand for talking straight, taking risks, and eschewing bureaucracy's dogmatic processes, while on the other being criticized as disdainful, condescending, and confrontational.

An articulate speaker and ardent advocate of education, Silber argued tirelessly for more spending on early childhood education and higher standards for teacher-training programs. In the tumultuous process of education reform, he calmly and consistently reminded the public that this is a gradual process which could take as long as a decade to show dramatic improvement. Silber believes that every child should be brought through the educational process to the highest possible level of achievement, but he says it is irresponsible to assert that all children can achieve at high levels, a claim that the board had made before he arrived (True Test, 1998). He is a supporter of vocational education, and he believes that any student who does not have intellectual interests should not necessarily go to college. For some, this is a refreshing opinion, since vocational programs in some Massachusetts towns have been under-funded or generally frowned upon due to widespread pressure to show high college attendance rates.

But Silber's outbursts at times undermined his own hard work; for example, in 1996 he surprised educators with a proposal to require high school seniors to take the GED exam to graduate. While this won the immediate support of several state officials, it was poorly thought out and he later retracted it after public outcry. Stunts such as this delayed the reform initiative; they not only alienated the public but also contributed to a communication breakdown on the board itself. Ideological differences on the board may not have been entirely Silber's fault, however. Former interim commissioner of education, Frank Haydu, III, said that next to widespread poor literacy skills, the contentious board of education, which was often unable to reach consensus, was the biggest obstacle to education reform (Education chief, 1998).

Reform Efforts: Curriculum Frameworks, Testing, and Charters

One of the first objectives of education reform was an effort to establish teaching and content subject standards in history and social sciences, English, mathematics, arts, health, science, and world languages. This was an arduous process that involved many people with diverging perspectives; the history and English drafts were particularly contentious, with much debate over political correctness and individual agendas. As a result, the final versions of certain frameworks were delayed by several years, which detracted from the time educators had to implement new curricula and prepare for state-mandated assessments. Complaints reflect considerable variation in thinking about teaching. Many of my colleagues in foreign language feel that the state's frameworks are too vague and broad, and instead prefer to rely upon the national standards. Social studies teachers, however, have complained that the frameworks are too specific; they resent the fact that the frameworks are taking away from their creativity, which is part of the fun of being a teacher. Students may lose the freedom to choose among the electives now offered in many schools, such as economics, law, or psychology, but it is felt by some that in the past eliminating electives has led to an overly narrow educational experience.

The frameworks were finally sent to schools after numerous delays, and although they are not mandatory, statewide testing will be based on the courses they recommend. But districts throughout Massachusetts have already invested significant resources in designing their own curricula. The state curriculum frameworks, they have noted, have not been evaluated as excellent, and many districts have not had adequate time to compare curricula and ensure that they are in alignment with state standards. As a result, when the first state exams were administered in 1998 (to establish benchmark scores), students in some communities were being tested on topics they had not studied (Boroschek, Oliff, and Tabor, 1998).

There is some skepticism about using the curriculum frameworks. This makes sense since teachers are fiercely independent and resent being told what to do. As a world language teacher, I agree with the frameworks and have always taught using the strategies they recommend. But when I am looking for inspirational ideas to enrich my professional practice, I seldom find myself turning to the frameworks. Nevertheless, teachers understood that the 1998 administration was the first go-around, and once the results from the MCAS exams were publicized, we would perhaps have more clear direction. As Jim McDermott of Worcester notes, even with the frameworks, "Curriculum is never finished. It is a continuing process, a dialogue involving everyone."

Once the frameworks were disseminated, the next step in education reform in Massachusetts involved testing all students and linking those results to graduation eligibility for tenth graders. The MCAS exams require annual testing of fourth, eighth, and tenth graders. Anxiety was high in May 1998, when the exams were given to 210,000 students for the first time, even though the results would not actually count towards graduation for another three years. After so much time and money had been spent on reform efforts, the exams had a certain Judgment Day quality to them; the expectation was that as many as 40 to 60 percent of the test-takers would fail. Indeed, it seemed that politicians and educators, including John Silber, spent more time preparing parents, teachers, and students for low test results than actually preparing them for the exam.

Parents and teachers want high standards and accountability, but many felt that the state acted hastily in giving the exams; the sample questions were released very late, and some principals were nervous that their curricula were not fully aligned with the curriculum frameworks. They complained they did not know enough about what the test would cover and what the stakes were. They noted that not only were the frameworks sent out late, but also that some English teachers, in particular, never received study guides to work on with their students to prepare for the written exam. The MCAS tests, which lasted up to 17 hours for tenth-grade students, were a mix of multiple choice questions and writing sections that required problem solving and thinking out answers. The MCAS exams have been criticized as taking too much time, thus displacing the curriculum, which had its biggest impact on advanced placement courses. The quality of the exams has also been widely debated. Of particular concern is the tenth-grade writing section of the 1998 exam, in which students were asked to comment on a selection from the short story "Good Country People" by the Southern Gothic writer, Flannery O'Connor. The story was intended as a prompt for students to write about the piece, but the poor wording of the question ("Based on these clues, write an essay that explains what comes next in this story."), caused significant confusion over whether students should "write an essay" that was analytical or write a creative piece about "what comes next in the story."

The quality of the exams and their administration, like the curriculum frameworks, will need to improve over time. There are questions around concerns such as validity and reliability, and the company that devised and graded the exams, Advanced Systems of Dover, New Hampshire, has already lost a multimillion dollar contract in Kentucky after botching the scores of a thousand middle school students (Jacoby, 1998). Teachers who were hired to score the exams during the summer of 1998 expressed dismay that the rubrics used to score the essays were not easily used with creative essays. "I felt I was compromising my standards to grade creative essays according to rubrics designed for analytical essays," said one participant. "The state needs to admit that students, and even teachers and administrators did not understand the question."

In some schools, teachers and administrators told students to write creative essays, while in others students were told not to be overly concerned because this first administration of MCAS would not count. Some of those students then spent valuable time drawing or writing about why these exams were a waste of time, and as a result those schools had lower overall scores when the results were released in November. The training received by teachers scoring the exams not only failed to address problems with the rubrics, but was also disturbingly devoid of a consideration of how issues of sexism and racism might affect the scoring. Scoring was not done blindly, and a few comments were made about the different writing characteristics of boys and girls, which caused me distress over how this might affect the reading of certain essays.

The state should recognize that there was a breakdown in communication somewhere along the way. Despite the publicity about the upcoming exams, many teachers, parents, administrators, and particularly, students were never given explanations about the importance of the exams; instead, they were just warned the results would be bad. Even though parents clamored for more accountability, it seems all sides needed a reminder of how important it was to seek high scores in these benchmark exams. In the future, the state must promote the exams as a positive experience, and it needs to ensure that not only are fair, reliable exams written for students, but also that all those involved in scoring them are sensitive to concerns that threaten objectivity.

The Massachusetts Education Reform Act of 1993 calls not only for student testing but also for prospective teachers and administrators to be tested for certification. Aspiring administrators have not objected to taking tests, although they have expressed concern over the quality of the proposed exams. Aspiring teachers, however, made Massachusetts a national laughingstock for their poor performance on exams when they were administered for the first time: close to 60 percent of the candidates failed, with 30 percent unable to pass a basic test in reading and writing. The failure rate in subject-matter tests varied from 63 percent in mathematics to 18 percent in physical education (Silber, 1998). While Silber laid the blame for poor results on schools of education, the state board of education seemed to lack a clear focus throughout the testing process. At first, prospective teachers were told the exam would not count, but then they were informed that it would; in the midst of that confusion, Silber felt there was no obligation to provide study guides for the exams.

Questions about the appropriateness of Silber's involvement in writing this teachers' exam also surfaced. Meetings between the testing company, National Evaluation Systems, and Silber occurred at Boston University, and included another board member who also was affiliated with Boston University. One of Silber's ideas, which was included in the exam, was a dictation portion using Federalist Paper No. 10. There is a clear conflict of interest in this since Silber is the chancellor of Boston University, which has a school of education. Critics have asked why a subcommittee was not involved in devising the test, rather than the committee chairman.

Despite questions about the exam itself, the results were an unmitigated embarrassment for stakeholders throughout the state. While schools of education have borne the brunt of jokes and finger pointing, the experience has also been demoralizing for dedicated educators statewide. Practicing teachers want to maintain high standards for their profession, but they have been angered and chagrined at the teacher-bashing and scapegoating that followed the release of teacher test scores in July, 1998. Silber has always been very critical of schools of education for what he regards as their inferior teacher-training programs with mindless courses and easy grading. With the release of the test results, he made it resoundingly clear that Massachusetts will not tolerate illiterate teachers. "One cannot teach what one does not know," he said (Silber, 1998). Regardless of whether or not a test is a good indicator of a person's ability to teach, any person who cannot pass a basic literacy test is not qualified to teach in Massachusetts. Most people agree with this point, although they would like to see it expressed in a more positive manner.

The landscape of educational reform in Massachusetts has changed dramatically with the introduction of charter schools, which were supported in the 1993 version of the reform legislation. They have been hailed as a panacea to traditional ills of public education, eliminating burdensome bureaucracy and contractual restrictions that have inhibited creativity and innovation in schools. While critics have attacked the charter school movement for destroying public schools, Massachusetts is indisputably at the forefront of the movement. The state has two types of charter schools—Commonwealth schools, which operate independently of the school district and are not necessarily bound by collective bargaining agreements, and Horace Mann schools, which are more closely controlled by local school districts and teachers' unions (Walker and Lehigh, 1998). Charter school supporters have cited the overwhelming parental satisfaction reflected in surveys, and they have noted that almost half of charter school students in Massachusetts are minorities, despite critics' warnings that such schools would segregate students. Supporters have also countered nay-sayers' assumptions that parents of charter school students were wealthier and more educated with survey evidence that showed 39 percent of charter school parents with incomes of less than $35,000.

Nevertheless, charter schools are still regarded with distrust by many educators in the state. While educators tend to agree that charter schools are innovative, they resent not only that money is taken from needy school districts in the process, but also that a growing number of these schools are managed by private, for-profit companies. Charter schools have received much attention in the press; indeed, they are a particularly hot topic for campaigning politicians. But many still regard them as a distraction from the real issue of improving teaching and learning: they serve only a small fraction of students in the state, they do not have a stellar track record with regard to disabled students, and they are still largely unproven, with no long-term record of success.

Accountability

Education reform efforts have sought to set high expectations and hold educators and students accountable, although achievement is not easy to measure. Studies have shown that teacher quality is the leading factor in student achievement, even more important than economic conditions. As the standards for teachers are tightened, the standards for students should then settle themselves over time. Several leaders, including Silber, have argued that just as lawyers and doctors are expected to pass rigorous exams, teachers, as professionals, must also meet tough state standards. Parents and taxpayers whose money is paying for education reform have a right to know that teachers are literate and competent in the subject matter they teach. Of particular concern in Massachusetts, especially in high school classes with high poverty rates, is the large number of teachers who do not hold college degrees in the subject areas they are teaching. Nationally, Massachusetts ranks 15th overall for having unprepared teachers in its secondary classrooms (Pressley, 1998).

The accountability debate has focused most sharply on schools of education. With the dismal test scores of aspiring teachers in July 1998, pundits and policy makers surfaced from all corners to denounce schools of education. Relegated to inferior status as an academic stepchild or cash cow by some universities, schools of education have not been dynamic leaders in the debate on school reform. They need to be more forceful in responding to boards of education and state political leaders. They have been criticized for lacking content and admitting students with low SAT scores, which Silber likened to an "open admissions policy." Colleagues of mine have voiced frustrations with the low quality of some of these courses, as well as the limited respect the schools sometimes have on campus and beyond. Policy makers have called upon schools of education to abandon or radically reform their current teacher preparation systems, since some students graduating from those programs are not competent to teach.

Boston University's school of education has been criticized for its attempts to screen students through its own exam (BU Test, 1998). The school notified students that if they did not pass the Boston University exam, the school would not sponsor them on the state teacher test. Their strategy has been described as a gimmick designed primarily to protect the university against the state's threat to shut down education programs with more than 20 percent of the candidates failing in two consecutive years. The students disclaimed by Boston University would appear as "unaffiliated" in the official results, and thus would not count against the school in the state's calculations.

Schools of education chided Silber for being narrow-minded in his ongoing tirade against them. Since only a small handful of students actually took the tests at certain schools, some of the data on failure rates have been exaggerated. They reminded Silber that the process of education reform involves aligning the curriculum at their schools to better prepare aspiring teachers to meet new standards; he should stop finger-pointing and begin working toward the next stage in this process. Finally, they have observed that programs already exist to recruit high school students and liberal arts majors to teaching, and yet they have not always been a resounding success. This is due to a more complex problem in our society, one that is inextricably linked to the high attrition rate for new teachers and needs to be addressed: too many teachers are isolated or unsupported in their work; they have to buy their own supplies or teach in rooms with broken windows and leaky roofs. Why are they not compensated and respected for the important function they perform?

Teacher compensation, along with the respect issue, has been raised as a key reason why more qualified undergraduates are not attracted to a career in education. Most practicing teachers I know argue that money is not a factor for them; they love working with children and are not dissatisfied with making less money than they might make elsewhere, although they do work very hard and resent the claims of talk-show hosts and columnists that they spend half the year on vacation. But it is indisputable that beginning teacher salaries ($26,000 with a bachelor's degree) are very low, especially in our strong economy. At the same time, we need qualified teachers more than ever: up to 40 percent of teachers in Massachusetts are expected to retire within a decade. Parents are quick to point out the difficulty in attracting motivated teachers at such low salaries, but where would the money come from? Unless the state came up with the money, raising teacher salaries substantially would involve increasing local property taxes, and that would be unpopular with taxpayers.

Responses to Reform

Teachers have generally been very supportive of education reform efforts, although they have been frustrated with an endless barrage of negative press, and with elected officials referring to aspiring teachers as idiots. Teachers want higher standards and accountability, but many are concerned that too much attention is being given to tests and not enough to the learning that is going on in individual classrooms across the state. The state tests have been particularly criticized as diminishing teachers' creativity and confining certain students to remedial courses to prepare for the tests; critics would prefer that the tests provide positive reinforcement, rather than threaten graduation eligibility.

Teachers have debated education reform *ad infinitum* in all venues: over lunch, at faculty meetings, at conferences, and at home. But, unfortunately, resistance to some education reform efforts negatively affected students' performance on the first administration of the state exams. As stated above, prompted by teachers' and parents' objection to the exams, some students either wrote essays protesting the whole experience, or did not take the exam seriously "since it would not count, anyway." In some schools this negativity was more covert but no less insidious.

When teachers criticized the exams or agreed with students' complaints that the test was unnecessary, they sent a clear message that such assessments are not consequential. As a result, the scores that those schools received were significantly lower. Administrators will need to address this before the next exam is given; they need to help parents, students, and teachers understand how state exams give the school a clear idea of how it is doing and in what areas it can improve.

While students have complained about the length of the state exams, they have generally responded well to education reform. Across the state, they are already showing improved test scores, especially in math and science. Scores have increased on state exams as well as national tests and exams, and students are taking higher-level courses in mathematics and science (Noyce, 1998). Administrators in school districts have tried to support this growth by expanding professional development opportunities for teachers, enabling them to integrate the frameworks into their curricula, and coaching teachers who may have low test scores. To prepare for the first administration of the exams, administrators held many informational meetings with parents and teachers, keeping the lines of communication open by sending letters home and allaying the fears of all those involved.

What do teachers need to make education reform work? Educators in Massachusetts would like to see more visible signs of public support and respect for their profession. Politicians and members of the board of education should seek them out and consider their first-hand knowledge of education reform. Teachers have supported the concept of exams, but many have warned that the 1998 exams displaced the curriculum and were too long, causing students to lose momentum. It is now the board's duty to act upon these reactions, and ensure that the release of student scores is framed in a constructive way so that communities may grow from the experience. The board should seek to avoid the debacle of the test results for aspiring teachers, which were released in a frenzied atmosphere with name-calling and laundry lists of low-performing schools of education. Teachers would also like to see some faith in the ability of schools of education to redesign their curricula and seek better-qualified education majors, especially among minorities, an area where there is a shortage of teachers.

Support from administrators is a key ingredient in making education reform work for teachers. Teachers want professional development opportunities to collaborate with each other and develop new curricula based on education reform. They want administrators to be vigilant in monitoring teaching and learning, with the skills to coach under-performing teachers, and the courage and endurance to remove them from the classroom if they fail to improve. Teachers value administrators who can communicate high expectations effectively and be responsive to their needs, as well as opportunities to influence their schools' policies on education reform.

Another cause of concern is the timing of the release of student scores. The exams take six months to score. While there is a large volume of tests to score, this is still a long time to wait for results. Releasing the results in November is unwise; its proximity to the fall elections adds more fuel to the political debate on the topic, and it leaves insufficient time to enact remediation programs before the administration of the next round of exams the following May. Administrators need to prepare and help teachers to respond to parents' questions and concerns about the implications of test results; even if the negative publicity continues, principals must think carefully and judiciously about the unique needs of their schools in light of the results.

Parental support is another crucial ingredient in the success of education reform. Surprisingly, despite the constant negativity surrounding educational issues, most parents support their schools and think teachers are doing relatively well. Parents agree with teachers in advocating high standards and supporting well-designed assessments that measure how their children are doing. But support is not the same as involvement, and many teachers lament that parents have not fully invested themselves in their children's education. Teachers and policy makers agree that literacy begins at home, and parents should play an important role in turning off the television, reading with their children, and getting them to do their homework. Silber has argued that the onus of implementing school reform is shared between parents at home and teachers in their classrooms, although achieving this balance is particularly difficult in cities where parental support is often inconsistent.

Teachers would like to see support from their peers through opportunities to share best practices and observe each other; they complain that administrators too often fill meetings with minutiae, rather than allowing time for sharing with colleagues. Teachers should call upon unions and professional organizations to help restore some of the respect that has eroded throughout this period. Unions, in particular, need to be more proactive in supporting reforms, lest teachers be seen as more interested in contracts and bread-and-butter issues than in raising standards for all. Some have seen politicians' disparaging remarks about educators as a stab at the powerful Massachusetts Teachers' Association (MTA). Teachers appreciate that the MTA has been a voice of reason amidst the hoopla about charter schools, and they encourage it to take a visible leadership role, helping all stakeholders to use the results of assessments to grow and improve practice.

The state needs to plan for the potential political and parental fallout when scores are released. Officials at the department of education have suggested that strategies such as summer school, stricter promotion rules for failing students, and teacher workshops may be employed for remediation. While other states have already gone through this process, policy makers are concerned with finding the right mix of reform ideas for Massachusetts. Communication from the board has been a problem in the past; even though teachers deal most directly with individual parents, news sometimes does not reach them until it has passed through a bevy of administrators. Improving the lines of communication is especially important with regard to the open-ended test questions; the scores for these are reported with explanations, some of which are vague, and teachers need support in using the results to meet the individual needs of all students.

Yet another concern, which some regard as a glaring omission in the discourse on education reform, is the large number of children in this state who go to school hungry every morning. Massachusetts generally has a good track record in protecting its children; it is the first in the nation in immunizing them and it provides for young people who are uninsured or have special needs. But the state cannot forget its 62,000 underfed children in the midst of the reform debate (McNamara, 1998).

Educators and taxpayers need to remind politicians that although teachers and schools of education might be easy topics for debate in an election year, they have an ethical responsibility to provide for the Commonwealth's hungry children.

Education reform continues to hold much promise for Massachusetts, but all sides must remember to maintain their long-term perspective, especially as the first results of reform-mandated assessments are released. People easily forget that this is a long-term effort; other states have had similar experiences with low scores the first time exams have been administered to students and prospective teachers. The significance of this time-span cannot be overstated; reformers need to fight against politicians' inevitable demands for quick fixes. The board of education should play a vigilant role defending its efforts, not allowing politicians to sidetrack or undermine reform efforts with irrelevant proposals or unnecessary diatribes against the profession. Such tactics have doomed many reform efforts in the past.

In addition to responding firmly to its critics, the board of education also needs to ensure that avenues for communication are wide open, especially between itself and the teachers and parents who will need to interpret the results of the tests. Administrators need to enlist the support of parents and also of education school professors in supporting good teaching, particularly in mentoring new teachers; increased contact with schools will enrich the experience of prospective teachers. The board also needs to remember that focusing on tests alone will not make for excellent schools; the MCAS exam, by itself, does not necessarily lead to better teaching in low-performance schools. Even the broad reform legislation has not satisfactorily addressed concerns such as high drop-out rates and aging buildings.

Education reformers in Massachusetts should maintain a positive perspective and remember the original objectives of this multi-year effort: to improve learning and instruction for all children in the Commonwealth, especially in poorer communities. This is particularly important because the reform legislation is such a comprehensive effort with so many noteworthy components. There have been poor test scores and misuse of public funds, but reformers must protect education reform from politicians' apocalyptic rhetoric about the decline of our schools. Education reform is a good thing that needs to be celebrated, yet we must ensure that a strong foundation is in place to guarantee its success.

On a Personal Note

Despite the intense, ongoing debate in the press and the political realm about the quality of education and teachers, most of the teachers I know are bright, dynamic educators who are dedicated to their work; they regard themselves as professionals and enjoy the respect of students and their parents. Some are angry at state politicians whose incessant squabbling and disparaging public statements have consistently belittled their hard work. Many parents who are in touch with the high-quality work going on in schools disregard the negative press, although this is not as easy for the many community members who do not have children in the public schools. Nevertheless, when such a large number of aspiring teachers in the state scores poorly on a basic literacy test, it leaves everyone wondering what is going on in our state's schools of education and in school districts willing to hire such candidates.

Standards play a significant role in my teaching and that of my colleagues. We have been leaders in the development and use of rubrics for holistic grading, for example, and we have often spoken at regional conferences on the innovative curricula we have developed. I rely upon both the Massachusetts World Language Curriculum Frameworks and the National Standards for Foreign Language Learning in developing curricula. (See National Standards in Foreign Language Education Project, 1996.) The national standards guide, a collaborative project of several national associations for foreign language teachers, is particularly useful. The standards hinge upon the catchy concept of five C's: communication, cultures, connections, comparisons, and communities. The five C's emphasize the importance of communicative proficiency, calling for foreign language classes to move away from focusing on grammar and vocabulary and, instead, to aim for students to acquire the ability "to communicate in meaningful and appropriate ways with users of other languages" (Standards, 1996). Access to technology, such as a multi-media language laboratory, is a key variable in this process. My students have used computers to edit videos in Spanish and produce sophisticated slide shows to present in class. The Internet has played an important role in researching and connecting with other cultures.

The Massachusetts World Language Curriculum Frameworks call for students to use language to connect to other disciplines and acquire information and knowledge. One of my colleagues and I have addressed this in two interdisciplinary courses we have developed, one on the history of Latin America and the other on the history of modern Spain. The courses, which are taught in Spanish and offered for credit in either social studies or world language, have been very successful with upper-level students interested in continuing their language study in a venue other than an advanced placement course. The two courses also represent an important development in the foreign language curriculum. Since the Massachusetts Curriculum Frameworks call for foreign language learning in grades K-12, students arriving at the high school level in future years may already be at a high level of proficiency. While they may then elect to study another language, many may opt to take advanced courses in the same language. Thus, it will be necessary to rethink the foreign language curriculum, developing interdisciplinary courses on foreign literature or art, for example, to respond to the interests of these students.

Not all districts in Massachusetts benefit from the resources, leadership, or sense of collegiality that we share in the community in which I teach. Regrettably, in many districts, opportunities for sharing and professional growth are infrequent. While teachers may have a chance to talk with colleagues at lunch or before or after school, time for such dialogue is unstructured and usually limited. Although I do not feel much isolation in my professional life, the overwhelming share of my time is spent with my students; I have never interacted with the foreign language departments in the communities contiguous to mine, and it has taken time to get a good sense of the unique activities going on in most of my colleagues' classrooms.

For the impatient, it is difficult to acknowledge that change takes time. For example, many teachers in Massachusetts are still adjusting to block scheduling. The extended time offers an exciting opportunity to develop new projects and change teaching styles, but the extra preparation involved sometimes means unexpected challenges, such as dealing with long lines at the copy machine. While I support high standards for teachers and students, I was disappointed by the first administration of the state exams. They should be written more carefully; they should take up less time; and the results should be released before the beginning of the next academic year to allow educators adequate time to study those results.

A final concern is the support that we particularly need to give nonprofessional status teachers. With so much negativity about the state's teachers and schools, along with salaries that are not always competitive, new teachers who have made it through the certification exams need encouragement and guidance. They might be paired with mentors through an organized mentoring system that meets regularly to talk about issues such as discipline or dealing with parents. Administrators play a key role in this process, since they need to be inducting new teachers, as well as guiding veteran educators in continuing their professional growth. Perhaps the state might expand its Attracting Excellence to Teaching Program, which offers partial reimbursement on loans for certain students. Teacher associations might consider lowering dues for new teachers, who are usually at the bottom of the salary scale.

Massachusetts educators have suffered considerable verbal abuse from politicians and reporters (and even their own education czar) during the past few years. But much of this has been election-year grandstanding, and the community members with whom my colleagues and I interact continue to support us unconditionally. High standards in schools and in schools of education will have the end result of strengthening educators' sense of professionalism and improving the quality of education for all students. There are no board of education panaceas; rather, improving education will take time, along with a commitment from a host of stakeholders.

References

Boroschek, J., A. Oliff, and D. Tabor. 1998. The promise and problems of the new statewide tests. *Boston Globe*, March 30.

BU test to screen teacher hopefuls, disclaim failures. 1998. *Boston Globe*, September 26.

Education chief quits after furor over tests; Acting Education Commissioner Frank Haydu says he doesn't want to get involved in election-year politics. 1998. *Boston Globe*, July 1.

Jacoby, J. 1998. Suspicions about the statewide tests. *Boston Globe*, May 7.

McDermott, J. (Personal communication.)

McNamara, E. 1998. Big talk leaves empty feeling. *Boston Globe*, July 15.

National Standards in Foreign Language Education Project. 1996. *Standards for Foreign Language Learning: Preparing for the 21st Century.* New York: Author.

Noyce, P. 1998. School reform working in math and science. *Boston Globe*, July 12.

Pressley, D. 1998. Study finds Bay State gives poor kids the worst teachers. *Boston Globe*, August 11.

Silber, J. 1998. Those Who Can't Teach. *Boston Globe*, July 7.

True Test; Silber gives ed-reform answers. 1998. *Boston Herald*, May 3.

Walker, A., and S. Lehigh. 1998. On charter schools, a split down party lines. *Boston Globe*, March 30.

7

VERMONT'S STANDARDS AND THE TEACHER ADVENTURE

by Patricia McGonegal

A diverse group of citizens assembled that morning in St. Albans. Some were teachers, some parents, some school board members, a few high-achieving students, and an administrator or two. I was facilitating a focus forum, designed as the first step in the structuring of a document important to the future of Vermont education: the Common Core of Learning. The brain child of Commissioner Richard Mills and his small but enlightened department of education, the Common Core was to be a joint effort by a cross-section of Vermonters, steered by a committee heavily laced with interested teachers like myself.

What we eventually drew up, at that and dozens of other focus forums, was a long, diverse list of skills, attitudes, concepts, and habits of mind that Vermont wanted for its students. Later, we categorized these lists into logical clumps of standards. A refined iteration of this list has come to be called the *Framework of Standards and Assessment*. This was my second experience with standards.

Portfolio Assessment: The Early Standards

A year before that, Vermont had begun exploration of a new assessment: the much-heralded Portfolio Initiative, which I also found myself part of. Portfolio Assessment began with standard setting. Groups of teachers collaborated on criteria for student writing, defining the criteria and articulating four levels of achievement for each, forming a one-page analytic scoring guide for student writing. These teachers then proceeded to assemble exemplary student work that would illustrate each level. These became, and have continued to be, the standards teachers began to use to teach writing to Vermont students.

Portfolio assessment held the same attraction for me as the Common Core standards-setting work, and as time went by, I found they were really different branches of the same reform. I was drawn by the authenticity of the endeavor. We were asking, "What are we doing in the classroom that looks like stuff people can really use out there in their lives?" But participation in both groups posed a common challenge: taking time out of my classroom added to my work, while understanding and cooperating with the administrators I worked with.

National Collaboration via New Standards

Involvement in standards and assessment work enabled me to understand the next chapter of Vermont's education reform history: the state's involvement in the setting and assessment of national standards. In the summer of 1991, some "portfo-lio" teacher-leaders were invited to attend two week-long conferences. At these meetings, researchers and reformers presented a theoretical base I found logical and useful, with elements of the ideas Vermonters had already espoused. These ideas, formed collaboratively by Vermont and a dozen other states, eventually formed a background for the standards movement in Vermont and across the country.

This was the summer the New Standards Project was born. Its directors were Marc Tucker, a reformer, and Lauren Resnick, a noted educator. Tucker pointed out the discrepancy between our beliefs and our practices: although we say that all stu-dents can learn and have equal access to education, we behave in our schools as if only a few can learn, and offer different degrees of access to them, depending on their status.

Resnick argued against the factory-like nature of our schools. She noted this irony: we know that learning is complex and dependent on diverse and individual needs, yet we run our schools as if knowledge were isolated bits of information that can be built onto students as if they were machines being processed on an assembly line.

Resnick and Tucker had had collective experience with reform, with teaching, with testing, and with international comparisons. Their joint conclusions focused on several elements:

1) Students in foreign schools achieve more than those in U.S. schools when they have a shared set of standards that largely drive their systems. Obviously, in schools in other nations these standards were clearly defined for all students.

2) Education in this country needs to move from the theory that some can be educated to the idea that all children can learn. This will require large-scale change.

3) If there is to be investment across our country, involvement is necessary by all the stakeholders at once: professionals from every level of U.S. schools, the business community, publishing companies, testing experts, curriculum developers, school administrators, representatives of higher education, par-ent groups, politicians, and teacher unions.

4) The three elements necessary to this change—standard-setting, instruction, and assessment—must be developed concurrently.

In their words, I heard the same passion for equity and revolution I had per-ceived in the philosophy of the Bread Loaf School of English during my four trans-formative summers there. I also heard echoes of the charge Rick Mills had issued when Vermont began its portfolio and framework programs: he called it the "Green Mountain Challenge: All children will reach high standards. No exceptions, no excuses."

Vermont and the New Standards Project began informed and complementary work, each moving toward the triune focus on curriculum, assessments, and instruction. This last intrigued me most as a teacher. It became clear to me that classroom practice must undergo real transformation if we were to address these standards with the commitment we owe every child.

The Key Ingredient for Standards-Based Teaching

In approaching this new set of challenges, a key change was a closer analysis of what students actually did in the classroom. Neither Vermont nor the New Standards Project invented this kind of analysis. I had often noticed the special education teachers at my school carefully analyzing their students' work. They were measuring habits of mind, attitudes, and learning behaviors long before state standards required such analysis. It was a mandated part of special education students' Individual Educational Plans (IEPs), and they were my first teachers in this area.

Researchers were analyzing student work as well. Don Murray at the University of New Hampshire and Miles Myers in California worked with "traits" they used to assess writing. Michael Armstrong, a Bread Loaf teacher and colleague, had written about analyzing the works of his primary school students. His *Closely Observed Children* was a handbook for this kind of careful examination. When I tried his program, however, I found it was extremely time-consuming to do this kind of analysis with many children.

Early Days of the Vermont Portfolio

Early portfolio efforts in Vermont introduced this analysis idea to teachers, and they shared my struggle to master the process. Some resisted the idea entirely. Why? It took time. It required aligning one's own internalized standards with the official ones. Analysis is work. Alignment is work. Change is work.

Another looming issue was—and still is—the translation of standards-based scores to traditional methods of grading. Some (mostly elementary) schools sidestepped this issue, designing a new system of reporting based on rubrics and standards-meeting, or reporting in a simple narrative form that stated teachers' observations and student strengths and needs. Others ignored standards-based data at report card time, and simply graded what was tested in the traditional way. And a third group dove into the job of rubric-to-grade translation: "An Extensively is an A, a Frequently is a B, etc."

A valuable device both researchers and practitioners learned to use was the benchmark. Slowly I learned that a piece of work was also a standard, a concrete "case" we could look at, just as doctors and lawyers use cases to model specific points, qualities, characteristics. Within the first few years, Vermont had published a booklet illustrating what a best, or worst, or in-between piece looked like, in reference to detail, or mechanics, or organization. This was our standard. This was something we could put our students' work up against. Again, this assumed the willingness of teachers to analyze and compare. In a subtle way, we were writing standards for other teachers as well. We were articulating what mattered and suggesting what level of work was going to be "good enough."

Portfolio Networks and the Challenge of Change

I worked with many Vermont teachers as they made their way through this process. The organizational plan for reaching teachers with information and professional development divided the state into networks of a few districts each. As network leader for the Burlington area, I could see clearly some positive and negative features of the program.

Positive Aspects

Teachers felt they could speak with some authority once they grasped the standards. They felt that when they spoke to a student about his or her work, their judgment or the guidance they gave represented a professional consensus. They were no longer judging their students' work with subjective and narrow criteria. The standards they were working with were clarified by the publication of ideas and benchmark pieces the department of education provided. Every student could have better access to clear articulation of what "good" writing was, and had a better opportunity to work toward producing this if he or she so chose.

Negative Aspects

There was, and remains, skepticism about possible unfair judgments of teachers based on generalized student scores. Teachers of "snapshot" year students (grades 5 and 8) bore heavily the weight of blame if a student's scores were not optimal, as many were not in those early years. Now that scored work was required to be included in their student portfolios, many teachers of English felt unduly burdened as well by having to become scorers and "correctors" of writing from other content areas.

Finding adequate time was and is an issue for teachers trying to learn something new. We complained about the change process: "Reforming schools is like repairing an airplane while it flies."

In My Own Classroom

I was lucky. Teaching sixth grade while these pilot years bore down on fourth- and eighth-grade teachers, I could pick and choose the elements and styles of assessment that suited me and my students. As far as standard-setting was concerned, I had already sorted through the elements of the framework; it was already my own. But it didn't belong to my students or to their parents, the two stakeholders I most needed to have engaged. When I begin my classes each year—in sixth grade and now in high school—I recreate a focus forum. I tape newsprint to my chalkboard and ask my students the same questions I asked in St. Albans that day: What should students know and be able to do by the end of this English class? Students show who they are and where they have been when they make their lists. Some talk plainly about wanting to read better or write effectively. Some give back the buzz-words their teachers have taught them. Some echo their parents. When Parent Night rolls around in the fall, I create the same process with parents, listing their common standards, then showing them what their sons and daughters have drawn up. After the listing exercise, I show both groups the lists the state has produced (the framework), draw parallels (and there always are parallels), and note gaps in either list.

In May, when my students have assembled a collection of writing, I ask them to collect samples from each of the forms of writing Vermont has required of its students. Sending home this collection, I elicit parent feedback on what they see as strengths and needs for each child. Parents are welcome to use the official rubric for scoring work, or just speak from their own set of standards. Feedback is gratifying, if disappointingly sparse. The involved parents look, and celebrate, and respond. The others, too threatened by school, teachers, or their own level of literacy, don't get into the conversation.

After ten years of this revolution, it's this idea of inequity that still challenges me most. It clearly is the focus of many current Vermont efforts. The legislature has passed a property tax reform law specifically aimed at equal education funding for every Vermont child. But the system grinds slowly. Those special education teachers are still analyzing student work, with bigger and bigger case loads every year. Educators who felt too uneasy to engage in the analysis still may be unwilling to join wholeheartedly in the reform efforts. And many children who still don't know what it takes to be a success will not know until it's too late. Have we helped lots of them with these initiatives? I don't doubt it. Have we still a long way to go? We have.

References

Armstrong, M. 1980. *Closely observed children.* London: Writers and Readers.

POLITICS, PEDAGOGY, AND PROFESSIONAL DEVELOPMENT IN MICHIGAN

by Laura Schiller

Recently, when my parents were in the market for a new home, my mom showed me the realtor's handout highlighting salient features for the prospective buyer. On top, a black and white photo putting the home at best advantage, below, the asking price, and right below the price, the school district's statewide testing or Michigan Education Assessment Program (MEAP) scores.

The importance of those state scores in determining property values and desirability comes as no surprise to Michigan teachers. We live under the hammer of statewide testing. MEAP scores drive school improvement plans, affect how classroom instructional time is used, and create a climate of pressure from school boards and superintendents, to administrators and teachers, that filters right down to the students.

When the state department of education approached the University of Michigan and the Michigan Partnership for New Education to put together a proposal for a federal grant that would fund new, integrated standards for English/language arts, there were those involved who saw this as an opportunity to influence statewide testing for the better. Here was the first chance in Michigan's history to bring together universities, the Michigan Council of Teachers of English, the Michigan Reading Council, the Michigan Association of Speech Communication, and the state department of education to rewrite standards reflecting current research in the field and progressive practice from classrooms across the state. In turn, these standards would drive future statewide assessments and, it was hoped, would lead to improvement in those assessments. In addition, many participants hoped the new integrated standards and benchmarks would contextualize the state tests, showing how limited a snapshot results from the MEAP tests, and building a strong case for valuing classroom- and district-based assessment.

There are great inequities in education in the state of Michigan. Inner city schools reel from poverty, fewer resources, and difficulty finding qualified teachers; suburban schools often reflect the benefits of greater resources—affluent population, bonds for technology, higher salaries to attract teachers, and newer facilities. Often the schools that face the greatest challenges in terms of student population find themselves with fewer support services, larger class sizes, and limited materials. In Michigan, statewide testing exacerbates the problems.

Poor performance on statewide tests points up disparities but does nothing to bring additional resources or help to those who need it most. Instead, high test scores drive up property values, while low test scores devalue property and demoralize teachers in noncompetitive districts, and they make it increasingly difficult to maintain a balance in the classroom between teaching solely for the state tests and teaching for a richer literacy.

My district, Southfield, is an example of a suburban district struggling to cope with a changing population and low MEAP scores. In recent years, there has been a large influx of African American and Chaldean students, the latter being Christians from Northern Iraq. With an increasingly diverse and transient student body (including many students for whom English is not a first language), finding ways to compete with nearby affluent districts continues to be a source of frustration. Every building has its MEAP plan, and every teacher and administrator is accountable. Scores are printed in local papers, and districts are judged by how well their students perform.

Will Michigan's new integrated English/language arts standards influence state tests as intended? Will teachers, in their quest to improve their state test scores, revise their classroom practice in light of the standards? As the tests are realigned with the standards, will they drive curricular reform and improve teaching and learning throughout Michigan?

Next year, Michigan will roll out a MEAP for social studies, a subject area that had not previously been tested. From all accounts, what is interesting about the test is that it is based on the new social studies content standards and benchmarks. As new assessments are written and old ones revised, it appears that the state standards are influencing the product. At the university level, the standards have also influenced conversations about teacher education and certification for English/language arts. Just how pervasive an influence standards will have in the future remains to be seen. But, in Michigan, some aspects of the standards work are unique and hold promise for improving teaching and learning.

Can Any Good Come of Standards?

For one thing, the collaboration between Michigan's professional organizations, universities, and the state department of education is a first in and of itself. Michigan's writing project and whole language educators were part of the conversation. Both research- and classroom-based, the standards were shaped by teachers for teachers, coming from the classroom—a different approach for the state. Hundreds of Michigan's teachers helped write the standards, lending a grassroots quality to the endeavor. Standards were a way to use more particularized language than we have had in past conversations to describe what our field is about. The standards gave teachers a way to talk about what we do as language arts educators so we could talk about ways we could grow. And while state politics played out through the state board of education did result in compromise, for the most part, the standards remained true to their original intent.

When the management team was planning the English/language arts standards, known as MELAF (Michigan English/language arts Framework), it was decided to include classroom examples, videotape, and narrative along with the standards. Awareness of the work many progressive teachers and districts were already engaged in around an integrated language arts curriculum led to the notion of demonstration sites—districts "where teachers might come together as an intensive study group in order to do three things: study the content standards in depth, examine their own teaching practices in light of these content standards, and observe how their teaching practices might grow and change as a result of this study (Casteel, Roop, and Schiller, 1996)."

The idea of a living curriculum built around the standards, supported by professional development and rich stories of classroom practice, and steeped in conversation and learning has proven to be a promising development. Four districts, already engaged in the work of integrated language arts and representing a wide range of students—rural, urban, diverse, homogeneous—and different socioeconomic strata, were selected as demonstration sites. Teams of twelve teachers from each site representing grade level clusters—K through 2, 3 through 5, 6 through 8, and 9 through 12—were identified. Southfield, my district, was included as one of the four demonstration sites.

Two summer institutes and regular meetings throughout two school years produced rich examples of student work and teacher learning. We studied each standard, examined our personal beliefs, made teacher research a way of life in the classroom, and set up goals and projects in our own classrooms and across our district teams to begin to enact the standards. We opened our classrooms and our voices to colleagues, guests, and parents; we saw MELAF evaluators and ourselves as standards pioneers, willing to take risks in our practice to re-envision teaching in light of the standards. We were on a journey that we willingly shared, but we always felt we had more questions than answers and believed that there would never be an end in sight.

The four demonstration sites are no longer funded through the original federal grant that sponsored the state standards project, but the progressive work and rich literacy results in those districts continue to grow. In the process of enacting the standards, the demonstration site teachers began to see themselves as models for the standards they were trying to bring to life in their classrooms. Two standards, in particular—6 and 10—had a dramatic impact on how teachers viewed their roles in their classrooms, with their colleagues, and in their districts at large.

Standard 6, labeled Voice, reads, "All students will learn to communicate information accurately and effectively and demonstrate their expressive abilities by creating oral, written, and visual texts that enlighten and engage an audience." The accompanying benchmarks that spiral from early elementary through high school include phrases such as: "Document and enhance a developing voice with authentic writings for different audiences and purposes." MELAF teachers modeled writing in their classrooms for their students, wrote about their practice for publication, and spoke about their practice before local, state, and national audiences. Clearly, they were finding their voice.

Another standard that had a major impact on the MELAF demonstration site teachers was content standard 10, labeled Ideas In Action, which reads, "All students will apply knowledge, ideas, and issues drawn from texts to their lives and the lives of others." Again, an accompanying benchmark, running through all grade levels culminates in high school with, "Utilize the persuasive power of text as an instrument of change in their community, their nation, their world. Examples include identifying a community issue and designing an authentic project using oral, written, and visual texts to promote social action."

When the state board of education politicized the standards and tried to reduce the conversation to a phonics versus whole language debate, it was the MELAF teachers and parents in their communities in chorus with business, university, and public school educators throughout the state who took political action and persuaded the state board of education to accept the standards. While compromises were reached, the heart of the standards remained intact and the MELAF educators learned invaluable lessons about coalition building and politics.

As the Michigan demonstration site teachers began to live the standards, they found themselves articulating their practice in different ways to different audiences. The Monroe demonstration site teachers, extended their ongoing participation in TAWL (Teachers Applying Whole Language) groups to host a Whole Language Umbrella conference in Windsor, Canada, and Detroit. They went on to take an active role in the 1997 National Council of Teachers of English national convention held in Detroit, which included on-site visitations to Monroe classrooms.

In Waterford, professional development opportunities continued with MELAF teachers taking a lead role in developing curriculum units in line with the state standards and facilitating study groups and workshops within and outside the district. In addition, several teachers from the demonstration site group took on different roles within the district, becoming principals and curriculum developers.

The Hillsdale demonstration site—a smaller, rural site—was led by its superintendent, who attended every meeting with his team over the course of two years. With strong administrative support, Hillsdale has watched its teachers take lead roles in curriculum, workshops, and district initiatives. Their work has resulted in a high school where the act of reading books in the hallway before school starts in the morning has become a socially acceptable pastime, where teachers are able and willing to articulate to their community how and why they teach the way they do, and where reading scores on statewide assessments are on the rise.

In Southfield, as with all the others, our story is still unfolding. When MELAF ended, Southfield's demonstration site teachers wrote a proposal to central administration asking to expand and continue our work with colleagues. Entitled SELAT, the Southfield English/Language Arts Team, we were given funding to enlarge our conversations about teaching and learning based on the state standards. With the help of Laura Roop and her husband, Dick Koch, both of whom had facilitated the demonstration sites for the state standards project, we planned and co-facilitated a year-long professional development initiative supported by administration that brought more of our colleagues into the conversation.

Several members of the MELAF and SELAT teams took on additional or different roles within the district. Some participated in a district think tank to help imagine where we might go from here in light of our district's strategic plan and curriculum frameworks. Others assumed staff development roles or became department chairs. Our district is now at the point where we are developing our local curriculum based on the state standards. Many of the MELAF and SELAT teachers have joined in the effort.

What Was Needed?

What was needed to make the standards viable in the demonstration site districts? What was needed to support teachers as they began to grapple with the standards in a way that enriched their teaching and student learning?

In Michigan, we've found that when standards are linked to professional development in the context of classroom practice, they can be an impetus for teacher growth and improved student learning. We've also learned that stories of teachers working to revise their practice in light of the standards can be useful in framing the conversation around standards. With that in mind, I'd like to take a closer look at how the standards pushed my classroom teaching and student learning. By sharing my story of intentionality in practice, I hope to tease out some of the issues inherent in standards work.

Intentionality: Meeting the Challenge of Standards in the Classroom

Demonstration-site teacher teams were asked to experiment with the standards. We were then expected to share student products, our resulting instruction, and reflections about the process with our colleagues both in and out of MELAF. Though I was an accomplished practitioner, my teaching and my knowledge of students grew when I allowed the standards to challenge what I thought I knew. I've learned there's no ceiling to what we can accomplish in the classroom.

Looking at the standards, I tried to imagine which I would focus on in the coming school year. One in particular stood out: Genre and Craft of Language. It read, "All students will explore and use the characteristics of different types of texts, aesthetic elements, and mechanics—including text structure, figurative and descriptive language, spelling, punctuation, and grammar—to construct and convey meaning." In our demonstration site work, we kept talking about "unpacking" the standards; looking at them in light of student work and what others in the field were saying, and rethinking our teaching as a result.

We'd learned that if you take a rich chunk of classroom practice and shake it, standards and benchmarks fall out. As one of many examples, we looked at a year-long inquiry into immigration I had conducted with my students. The culminating project was a whole-class publication called *Coming to America*, written by parents and students and published in whatever language they felt most comfortable in using. Parents were then invited to come to class and read their pieces and receive responses. In my multicultural setting, the purpose was to honor the home language while understanding the language of education and commerce in our society today. I also hoped through our stories to build community and a deep appreciation and respect for all members of our classroom and our world. I believed if we could start with our own stories, we could come to know the stories of others across time and place.

Many standards were evident in our student publication. Based on the labels we'd given to our standards, it was easy to see an emphasis on and evidence of meaning and communication, language, literature, voice, depth of understanding, ideas in action, and inquiry and research. When I looked closely at our *Coming to America* class book, however, I realized that almost every piece was as a personal narrative.

My teaching was organized thematically. While we looked in class at some elements of the writer's craft (leads, strong verbs, figurative language, dialogue), I became uncomfortable wondering just how much I knew about teaching a specific genre. After more than twenty years of teaching, I was questioning the depth of my understanding about the standard called Genre and Craft of Language.

I decided to make that standard the focus of my teaching for the coming year, but I had no idea how to proceed. In *Living Between the Lines*, Calkins (1991) talks about memoir as a "window on our lives" and "emblematic moments" that help us understand who we are. . . . "When we write memoir, we must discover not only the moments of our lives, but the meanings in those moments" (p.177). This was for me. I wanted my students to find meaning in their lives and to appreciate and respect the lives of others by sharing all our stories. I thought about my impulsive sixth graders who acted first and thought later, whose world was walled in self-conscious mood swings and focused inward. I wanted to find ways to help my students become more reflective, deeper thinkers—to move from the concrete to the abstract—to become more caring individuals.

In memoir I saw the possibility of honing my practice to improve not only my students' grasp of literacy, but also their depth of understanding of themselves and others. My intent was to study the genre of memoir and experiment with it in my classroom, then apply what I learned to other genres. At a loss for how to begin, I decided to read some memoirs to get a feel for the genre. In the summer when I had time, with titles suggested by friends, I read several book: Mikal Gilmore's *Shot in the Heart*; Henry Louis Gates, Jr.'s *Colored People: A Memoir*; *The House on Mango Street* by Sandra Cisneros; poetry by Jean Little and Eloise Greenfield; Faith Ringgold's *Tar Beach*; Mildred Taylor's *Roll of Thunder, Hear My Cry*; and "Letter from a Concentration Camp" by Yoshiko Uchida. When I looked, memoir was everywhere, in the bookstores and on my own shelves. I'd just never noticed before.

I began with *Shot in the Heart*, the story of Mikal Gilmore's search to understand what led to his older brother Gary's life of crime and ultimate execution. Through Gilmore's eyes, I saw memoir as a compelling need to retrace and make meaningful those moments and events that shape our destinies. From Henry Louis Gates, Jr. I learned the importance of time and place to memoir. In the preface to *Colored People: a Memoir*, he explains that he wrote the book for his daughters so they will understand the "world into which I was born (p. xi)" and "why we see the world with such different eyes (p. xvi)." Gates recreated his childhood during the 1950s and '60s in Piedmont, West Virginia. I felt invited into his family. Knowing the people in his life, their humor, their struggles, their ideas, made me more willing to hear other points of view, and I wondered if my students would be more receptive to other points of view as a result of reading memoir.

The House on Mango Street is a series of vignettes written in poetic prose about a young Hispanic girl growing up in Chicago. Cisneros's use of imagery, details, and the senses, and her ability to find meaning in what we often take for granted pushed my understanding of craft and the power of memoir to connect with our everyday lives. I contrasted Cisneros's vignette entitled "Hairs" with Gates's chapter "In the Kitchen." Both authors wrote about the same subject in different ways. Both chapters resonated for me, the once awkward teenager who wore orange juice cans topped by a babushka on a trip to humid Miami rather than suffer the indignity of frizzy hair. Later, in a sublimely teachable moment, I used both pieces with my students after my student Meloni taped a swatch of her hair to a page in her writer's notebook in anguish over a new hairdo and shared her entry with the class.

As part of my summer preparation, I tried writing a memoir in my own notebook. I felt I had to experience what my students might experience in order to be an effective writing coach. To get the feel of memoir before bringing it to my students, I started listing emblematic moments in my life, just as I imagined asking my students to do. Using freewrites, I wrote of each moment, noticing connections, recurring themes, oft-mentioned relatives. My emotion caught me off guard, and more than once I found myself laughing or crying as I relived important moments in my life. Would my students experience the same intensity of feeling? Could I create a safe enough classroom climate that would be conducive to writing about those things that matter the most to us?

When Student Work Mirrors Teacher Learning

When it came time to begin our class memoir study, I read aloud three examples of memoir without labeling them as such. The first chapter from Patricia MacLachlan's young adult novel, *Journey*, Faith Ringgold's picture book, *Tar Beach*, and "Growing Pains," a poem from Jean Little's *Hey World, Here I Am!* I asked students to freewrite and reflect on what these pieces had in common. When we shared our freewrites, Kerry noticed they all dealt with family. Kevin said they were all about people relating to each other. Ryan commented that one person seems to be telling the story.

I talked about memoir, what I'd read over the summer and how I experimented with memoir in my writer's notebook. I told how memoir helped me understand myself better as I learned to understand others. Using Gates as an example, I told how memoir helped me look back on my life and find moments that led me to new insights and made my life meaningful. I showed my journal, mentioned my camp and family stories, and held up several of the memoir books I'd read over the summer. Then I passed out a letter to take home inviting parents and students to write for a class memoir book. I explained I would be writing, too, and we would celebrate publication with a book signing at our local Borders Books.

We immersed ourselves in memoir. We tried writing in our notebooks about emblematic moments in our lives. We experimented with memory maps as a way to tap into our lives. We looked for connections between our entries. We studied ways different authors approached memoir: Uchida's "Letter from a Concentration Camp," written by a Japanese-American boy to protest his internment during World War II; a short story from Gary Soto's *Small Faces* entitled "The Jacket," an example of how an object can drive memoir and how that jacket, "the color of day old guacamole," (p.37) came to represent all the misery and insecurity of sixth grade; the picture book, *Uncle James*, in which author Marc Harshman deals with the pain and disappointment of alcoholism in a family; and on and on. Sometimes I'd bring in a special text to share; sometimes the sudents brought a text to the attention of the class, as when Eric shared *Pink and Say* by Patricia Polacco, which deals with the Civil War, death, and race.

For our purposes, we broadened the notion of memoir to include fictionalized texts that had strong elements of memoir. That made many more texts available to my sixth graders. We also talked about the author's prerogative to fictionalize, change an ending, make it the way you would want it to be, imagine what you can't remember. The telling is the author's; by making explicit to students that authors sometimes fictionalize, I could enable students writing about difficult moments in their lives to write themselves to a safe place. There was an escape clause.

Writer's craft became an increasingly prominent feature in my lessons and in our classroom writing and reading experiments. From Barry Lane's *After the End* we borrowed the notion of snapshots, thought shots, and dialogue as integral parts of text. We used the method of copysearch to find examples in the memoirs we were reading, and we revised some of our writer's notebook entries using snapshots, thoughtshots, and dialogue. We studied leads that made us wonder and drew us in. We searched for leads we liked in our readings and revised our own leads. We tried to slow down important moments, use strong verbs, picture our sensory images, and craft realistic-sounding dialogue. The writing that resulted was richer, had more voice, and showed a greater command of language than was evident in our *Coming to America* class book from the previous year. We progressed from passages like Clarence's, fairly typical of our earlier publication:

> Clayton lived in Chattanooga, Tennessee. He was sent to Ypsilanti where my grandmother lives because he was ill and his sister couldn't take care of him. He lived in Ypsilanti for three years before he died. He was very tall and proud. His hair was jet black and curly. He reminded you of a big Indian Chief...

We ended with "Lights," written by Jocelyn, representative of the caliber of writing evident in our class memoir book. Our writing became more literary as we studied genre and craft.

> South Bend, IN—
> Over at Aunt Sheila's house we'd catch lightning bugs. The summer nights were cool and calm, the sun half hidden—just enough light to cast orangey glows where it hit, turning usually "innocent" things into monstrous shadows...

"Memoirs," years two and three, found me branching out and attempting to explore poetry in much the same way I'd explored memoir. I'd been keeping company with poets who convinced me that poetry is the heart of all language. My repertoire of writer's craft expanded to include paring down language, using appositives, alliteration, and metaphor; working an image into a poem; using old words in new ways; writing for surprise; using 3's, lists, participial phrases; juxtaposing text; and working with deep revision techniques, all of which I experimented with in my own writing and discovered in my personal reading in the process of coaching my students.

I used the same rich exploration of texts with my students, reading, writing, sharing, revising, searching through our reading again and again for examples of craft and experimenting with our own writing as a way to try on the writer's craft. My teaching was now shaped by genre studies, poetry, memoir, and expository text, instead of thematic studies, for I found I was not yet proficient enough to handle both at the same time. The result: student learning mirrored teacher learning. A typical entry from this year's sixth-grade class book of memoir is represented by Carmen's "A Special Relationship."

...Tata jumped and dropped his knife to the floor. He ran to see what happened, but all he saw was a little girl on the floor, tangled like the sweater in the corner of her bedroom, smiling up at him.

"Well since you're falling over to eat some peanut butter and banana sandwiches, you can have the bigger half." The smell was so thick, almost like a fog of peanut butter.

"Now get back up on the couch." He sat down, making my half of the couch puff up.

"If your Baeli sees sneaker marks on the furniture we'll be eating in the kitchen until you graduate high school."

I came and sat on the puff and watched the ball game.

"Tata, are the Yankees the best team in the league?" I asked staring up at him, even though I knew the answer.

"Si, Carmen. The Yankees are numero uno."

All year Carmen read like a writer. She saw herself as an author, revising and crafting her words to meet the standards of published literature. Carmen has a record of academic success. She would probably achieve in any academic setting. Not so, however, for the majority of students I teach. B.J. stands in contrast to Carmen.

For all his elementary school years, B.J. was labeled "special education, learning disabled." He represents the diversity and success of our sixth-grade classroom authors. In his first year out of special ed, B.J. found his voice as a writer.

THE HOLY BAG

My bag is coming apart like Mr. Potato Head. In fact, I have to attach the tongue of the bag to the arm of it leaving a huge knot with threads jetting out like quills of a porcupine. Some parts of my bag have massive patches. Its white, black, and blue colors seem a little faded.

My bag looks like it's been mauled by a rottweiler with holes the size of golf balls. It smells like outside after it showered with rain. I do not really want to ask my dad for a new schoolbag knowing that he will put it off and say, "Maybe later," meaning later in next month?

"Can I have my schoolbag now?" I asked as I traced his steps down the stairs dragging my schoolbag down behind me with a gap the size of a black hole...

So much of B.J.'s competency mirrors my learning. During our study of expository text, B.J. chose to research NASA's space program. He began his paper, titled "Journey to Discovery" with, "What draws us to the unknown? How can we quench this thirst of conquest, building vehicles to the stars?" Engaged in a self-selected topic that mattered to him, supported by multiple sources, and reading not just for information but also for craft—all these gave B.J. the tools to attempt the literary. His standards for excellence, his models, were the articles from *Newsweek*, NASA, and *National Geographic*, all sources traditionally too challenging for most sixth graders.

I used to read Nancy Atwell and Linda Rief and skim over the student work in their books. My writing project director drew my attention to the quality of their students' reading and writing. That was a wake-up call; but without a close study of Genre and Craft, my students' products could never have approached their present quality. At a time in my district when the demographics are in flux, I often hear the teacher-code statement, "It isn't like it used to be." As if to say, "You can't expect as much from these students," or, "They're not as capable or motivated as their predecessors." Yet I've been able to document consistently over time the highest quality student work I've ever seen from my Southfield students, a direct result of my learning. In their preface to *What's Worth Fighting for in Your School*, Michael Fullan and Andy Hargreaves (1996) write,

> It is a time for teachers as impassioned moral change agents to fight for the positive preconditions that will shape the profession for the next era: an era in which the learning of teachers will become inextricably bound to the learning of those they teach. (p. xiii)

If we, as educators, recognize this reality, will it be enough to improve learning for our diverse student population?

Building a Common Language of Practice

The Center on Organization and Restructuring of Schools (CORS) analyzed data from 1,500 elementary, middle, and high schools at various stages of restructuring. Their conclusions value teacher learning but acknowledge the limitations as well.

> We saw schools with competent teachers that lacked the organizational capacity to be effective with many students (Newmann and Wehlage, 1995, p. 29).

The CORS message to schools is clear. Creating a professional community raised student achievement across socioeconomic groups. However, they note this caution:

> If schools want to enhance their organizational capacity to boost student learning, they should work on building professional community that is characterized by shared purpose, collaborative activity, and collective responsibility among school staff. (p. 37)

I was fortunate to have been part of the conversation from the inception of the English/language arts standards. When the demonstration sites were selected, once again I was involved with sustained, meaningful professional development opportunities with colleagues from within and outside of my district. But it has since become clear to me that though my practice and that of my MELAF colleagues has grown, in order to improve the quality of learning for many more of our students, we must work to build a professional community in our buildings.

CORS also refers to state standards as an external influence for high quality learning. It is interesting to note the authors' observation:

> . . .though. . .those schools that made the best use of such standards were already inclined to see the need for them. . . staff were motivated to search for help and to draw ideas and insights from external resources about standards and how to put them into practice (p. 43).

I was receptive enough to the standards to perceive that I had much to learn, but I know many teachers who look at the standards and, in effect, say, "been there, done that." I put aside resistance and doubt and set about looking closely at student products with an eye toward intentionally and systematically improving practice. But I'd been the beneficiary of numerous professional development opportunities prior to my standards work. Not all my colleagues have been as fortunate or as willing or able to put in the extra hours of study it takes to improve practice in the ways I've described.

If districts plop standards down in front of teachers without ongoing professional development grounded in classroom practice, the standards will remain words on a page. Without sustained professional development to accompany the standards, we will reduce our teaching to the bits and pieces of discrete skills, specific language, and prompts that on the surface appear to comprise our statewide tests. With rich conversations, readings, systematically experimenting with standards in the classroom and revising practice in light of new learnings, Michigan's MEAP test preparation could take on a richer guise.

When school districts, teachers, and parents begin to view statewide assessments as only one snapshot of competency and districts begin to give higher priority to multiple assessments grounded in the classroom and in district initiatives, perhaps the political overtones of statewide testing can be muted. Perhaps a balance can be reached between rich classroom practice, teacher learning, and student growth, and the pressure to reduce what we most value in education to a single battery of tests and the preparation they entail.

Several communities in Michigan have experienced parent and student revolt over the state High School Proficiency Tests. Parents have boycotted the tests fearing their children's college admissions records could be damaged if their children scored poorly. In these districts, students have traditionally scored well on ACTs and SATs and been accepted into highly regarded universities. With other measures of assessment available against which to evaluate the quality of their public schools and individual achievement, parents and students alike have viewed the state tests as risky and unnecessary to improve education.

Perhaps as school districts articulate to their communities the limitations and alternatives to statewide high-stakes testing, parents and teachers will feel less pressure from the state-mandated politicized tests, as has happened in some of our more affluent districts. Perhaps we can begin to couch assessment in a broader context, one that places additional value on classroom assessment and individual student growth. Perhaps we can begin to view assessment as linked to professional development, using the standards as a way to recognize, label, and experiment with improving teaching and learning.

Standards have the potential to help teachers collaborate and begin to label their practice so the work of improving teaching and learning can be enhanced. Standards have the potential to improve the depth and quality of statewide assessments and inform teacher education and accreditation requirements. Standards have the potential to support the need for professional conversations about literacy and research-based practice. But, standards also have the potential to remain empty words, ignored in the blizzard of mandates—state, district, and building—that blankets the reality of classroom teachers' lives today. At best, standards are a portal; whether we choose to enter will be decided, teacher by teacher, district by district, state by state.

References

Calkins, L. 1991. *Living between the lines.* Portsmouth, N.H.: Heinemann.

Casteel, J., L. Roop, and L. Schiller, 1996. No such thing as an expert: Learning to live with standards in the classroom. *Language Arts, 73:* 30-35.

Cisneros, S. 1989. *The house on Mango Street.* New York: Vintage.

Fullan, M., and A. Hargreaves. 1996. *What's worth fighting for in your school.* New York: Teachers College Press.

Gates, H. L., Jr. 1994. *Colored people: A memoir.* New York: Alfred A. Knopf.

Gilmore, M. 1994. *Shot through the heart.* New York: Doubleday.

Greenfield, E. 1998. *Nathaniel talking.* New York: Black Butterfly.

Harshman, M. 1993. *Uncle James.* New York: Cobblehill Books.

Lane, B. 1993. *After the end: Teaching and learning creative revision.* Portsmouth, N.H.: Heinemann.

Little, J. (986. *Hey world, here I am.* Toronto: Harper Trophy.

MacLachlan, P. 1991. *Journey.* New York: Delacorte.

Newmann, F., and G. Wehlage. 1995. *Successful school restructuring: A report to the public and educators by the Center on Organization and Restructuring of Schools*. Madison, Wisc.: Wisconsin Center for Education Research.

Polacco, P. 1994. *Pink and say*. New York: Scholastic.

Ringgold, F. 1991. *Tar beach*. New York: Scholastic.

Soto, G. 1986. *Small faces*. New York: Dell.

Taylor, M. 1976. *Roll of thunder, hear my cry*.

Uchida, Y. 1990. Letter from a concentration camp. In A. Durrell & M. Sachs (Eds.), *The big book for peace*. (pp. 57-61). New York: Dutton.

9

OBSERVATIONS OF A NOVICE TEACHER IN NORTH CAROLINA

by John Walsh

I began teaching at a middle school in 1991 after completing a successful military career. On the one hand I was leaving an institution famed for its chain of command, and on the other I was joining the loosely knit confederation of educators.

My military training stressed the value of being goal-oriented and following orders. But during my initial year of teaching I was surprised to learn that teachers had tremendous power to decide the curriculum on their own behalf. In other words, it was almost solely up to me to decide what to teach, how to teach it, and when to teach it. Teachers were not given a master lesson plan and told to follow it. Many administrators played only a subordinate role in this decision-making process, because the teachers were expected to prepare and deliver the curriculum in an efficient manner. But common sense kept telling me that there must be a source document or a curriculum bible, so to speak.

When I finally located a copy of the North Carolina Standard Course of Study in my principal's office, I was told by a fellow teacher that nobody really paid any attention to it anyway, and that I would be wasting my time even reading it. But contrary to that advice, I began to read it and soon realized that it was indeed the state's battle plan for seventh grade.

I was disappointed, however, to note that the majority of my colleagues were neither interested in, nor concerned about, the state curriculum. In defense of those teachers, I must say that most of them were teaching relevant subject matter and doing a pretty fair job of it. Oh, there were rumblings that a particular teacher was doing a really good or a really poor job, but we were unable to verify such claims since there were no overall standards. Teachers exercised their classroom autonomy, and as we all know, it is difficult to compare apples and oranges.

But change was on the horizon, for within a year state testing would work its way into our cozy local school communities and upset the balance that had prevailed for so long. Suddenly teachers no longer possessed the almighty power to create the final exams that their own students would take. The test, instead, would be created in Raleigh, by people who were not even teachers, and it would be administered statewide!

The Origins of State Testing

I clearly remember my first encounter with state testing in 1993. After school on that first test day, many teachers were lamenting the test and forecasting doom and failure for their students. Some of them seemed mystified at the breadth and depth of the test questions, and they spoke of a strategy to shift any potential blame onto the students.

I had no comment at this point because I was still a novice teacher. I had invested substantial time reviewing the goals and objectives of the state curriculum throughout the year, and I felt as though I had properly prepared my students for the test. This really wasn't much different from getting prepared for a military inspection, and I was confident as we awaited the test results.

Both of my math classes had been able to complete all the lessons in the math book, even if my regular math class had to "skim" the last four chapters. All in all, the students had exerted a good effort, and I anticipated above-average results from them. But this was really a blind prediction; we had never taken state tests before, and there were no standards or benchmarks against which to measure our efforts.

As teachers began talking about the test and gossip began to swirl about the school, I was surprised at what I was hearing. The general tenor of comment addressed itself to the unfairness and irrelevance of the test. Other criticisms focused on the outrageous manner in which the state had "violated" the sanctity of the teacher's classroom, and dared to check up on our students via a state test. But I tried to remind my colleagues that we were all licensed and employed by that same state.

Personally, I didn't see any conflict with the action of the state. But remember, I was trained to accept direction from above, and I had "cheated" (as I was later accused) by looking at the state course of study and using it to help prepare my students for the test.

As more information filtered back from my colleagues, I suspected that they were really just reacting against the change that testing was creating. No longer would they be the sole masters of their classroom domains. From here on out the state would dictate a course of action that would forever change the way in which teachers lived their lives.

When the last after-shock of the testing experience began to dissipate, we began to speak our true thoughts and feelings more openly. One trusting friend told me that she was only able to cover the first eight chapters of the 14 in the math book, and much to her utter dismay, most of the test covered material from the second half of the text. She quickly assumed a defensive posture and stated that she would have been able to cover the entire book, had it not been for a few "chronic troublemakers" who were no doubt responsible for keeping the class off-task.

Another friend was quick to point out that most of her students did not have sufficient time to complete the test, and those that did complained that the questions really made them think. A third colleague indicated that her students seemed somewhat bewildered by the calculator and protractor that were provided for the test. She had noticed her students wasting time, apparently trying to figure out how to use these two resources.

When the test results finally did come back, the students at our school were judged to be about on par with other students in our state, but the entire state report card showed the need for growth. Some students did well; others did poorly. With the published results in hand, teachers were now able to compare class scores and evaluate student performance for themselves. Since the students were tested in their homeroom environment, test scores were likewise reported. I found it amazing that a social studies teacher would brag about students in his homeroom doing so well, when an English teacher was criticized because her homeroom students did poorly. It is worth remembering that neither of these teachers really had very much to do with the math instruction for their students.

The Beginning of Reform in North Carolina

Like educators in every other state in the union, North Carolina educators want to improve the public's perception of their educational system. The issues surrounding these considerations are very real and powerful. State economies tend to be fueled by an educated work force. An abundance of educated and skilled workers has a tremendous impact on a state's ability to attract manufacturing and business.

Our state began to take a serious look at this situation when a recent national study concluded that North Carolina was ranked near the bottom of the nation's public education systems. This was not a very enviable position to be in, but at least there was much room for improvement!

I personally questioned the validity of those rankings in the absence of national standards. If memory serves me correctly, they were based on SAT scores; but states vary in how many students take the SAT. A higher-than-average percentage of our students took that test, while only a more select group of college-bound students took the test in some of our sister states. So, first and foremost, if you must have tests, the tests must be fairly administered and invalid comparisons avoided.

Any teachers beyond their first semester of teaching will be quick to surmise what happened next. That's right, the teachers were blamed for the dismal performance of the students. Poor performance on the SAT equated to poor teaching.

But North Carolina teachers were quick to defend themselves by pointing out that teacher pay in our state ranked right alongside student test scores—near the very bottom! While there is certainly no empirical evidence of a cause-and-effect relationship between teacher pay and student performance, the correlation appeared obvious, and the teachers had made their point.

The ABCs of Public Education

In response to these and other criticisms of its public education system, North Carolina's general assembly passed the School-Based Management and Accountability Program (SB1139) in June 1996. In response to that legislation, our state board of education developed the ABCs of Public Education.

The ABCs focus on strong accountability with an emphasis on three components: high educational standards; teaching the basics; and maximum local control. Specific detailed information about the ABC Plan will be presented later in the chapter, but for now, suffice it to say that the plan envisioned increased teacher pay for increased student achievement.

As we now prepare to enter our third year of the ABC Plan for grades K through 8, a number of interesting observations come to mind. The views and opinions that are shared in this chapter have been accumulated through various unofficial means, including: personal contact with teachers in my district, discussions at graduate school with teachers and administrators of surrounding districts, and reports of interviews published in various newspapers and other public forums. These observations are presented to share the feelings of North Carolinians (including parents and students) regarding accountability and state testing—but, obviously, they represent my own interpretations.

End-of-Grade Testing

In 1996, the first year of End-of-Grade (EOG) testing, I was teaching at a middle school populated primarily by minority students. The school had a reputation for unruly and disruptive students, and many teachers (myself included) were requesting transfers. Shortly after the school year ended, I received a telephone call from the new principal inquiring as to why I had requested a transfer. Without getting into specifics, I told him that I thought we needed a complete make-over at the school. He asked me whether or not I thought the students at that school could learn, and of course I said they could, and I really meant it. I told the new principal that I would not withdraw my request for transfer, but if it wasn't approved, I would be happy to work with him. Actually, I rather hoped the transfer wouldn't be approved; and it wasn't.

I remained at that school, beginning what would prove to be a remarkable journey from the "school with *those* kids" to an Exemplary School, that very same year.

The first strategy we implemented was the power of believing. This was not some fancy formula spread by gurus traveling around the country, hawking for five thousand dollars a pop. We just began to create a vision that our students were as good as any other students in the state, and that they could achieve "reasonable growth."

Some of us were afraid to believe that we could make it happen. We knew what to expect because the end of course tests from the 1995-96 school year were going to be the benchmark from which we would measure student progress during that first year of state testing, as mandated under the ABC Plan. But this task seemed almost insurmountable to some of our staff.

Many decisions made by our administrator surprised us. He let me teach sixth grade with a self-contained class. This is what I had requested during our conversation that summer, but I really didn't expect to get it. He let teachers team with partners of their choice (for the most part) and required nine-week lesson plans, rather than daily or weekly plans. He also encouraged diverse teaching styles and strategies. And, perhaps most importantly, he thought of us as professionals. He treated us as such, and expected us to act as professionals.

Our faculty and students worked very hard during the 1996-97 school year. Much to the utter amazement of nearly everyone in our district, we were designated an Exemplary School. Each teacher also received a $1,000 bonus from the state.

The next year we improved our battle plan and again achieved exemplary status, missing a School of Distinction designation by a mere two one-hundredths of a point. The reason I share this happy story is that I was there and have first-hand knowledge of what was accomplished and how it was accomplished. I guess you could say that I was an early supporter of our state testing program.

As we begin our third year of end-of-grade testing, and strive for ever-increasing levels of student achievement, I have begun to ponder some of the points previously raised by others with whom I have had professional discussions. I certainly have not abandoned my almost endless belief that all students can learn, but I have noticed a slight tarnishing of the luster on the "standards and accountability model" for the state of North Carolina.

Critical Views

Some of the most vociferous criticism of state testing involves the notion of test validity. We are currently using multiple choice tests for math and reading in grades 3 through 8. One of the major objects of criticism is the multiple choice format, rather than assessments that would provide more authentic data.

That brings to mind the difficulty we have encountered with our state writing test during the last two years. Writing tests are mandated in grades 4 and 7, but they have been given in other grades as well for diagnostic purposes. Students are given a prompt and are told to respond using one of the prescribed styles of writing (point-of-view, descriptive, narrative, etc.) For whatever reason (and I am not faulting the state in any way) the tests were sent out to an agency that had been contracted to grade them. When the scores finally came back, teachers were flabbergasted (and in my opinion rightfully so). The grades were dreadful, and there appeared to be a serious lack of consistency in the grading process. Most teachers simply could not accept the fact that their best students, the ones most prepared for the test, had scored such low grades. We are still at a loss to determine how there could be such a disparity between our efforts and our results. So much for open-ended tests!

The State's Accountability and Standards Program

As mentioned earlier in this chapter, North Carolina has invested approximately 10 years in a program of educational reform that has resulted in the state showing one of the highest sustained rates of improvement in student achievement in our nation.

The first state test used end-of-course scores from 1995 to establish baseline data for the elementary and middle schools. During the 1996-97 season, those scores were also used to determine the required growth for student achievement. It was decided that expected growth from one grade level to the next should be represented by approximately five points' improvement on the test.

Actually this standard varies from year to year, and this variation is one of the issues that drive teachers crazy. Many of them suspect that the standards may be manipulated after the tests are scored. While I have seen nothing to indicate that this is happening, the mere perception of it shows a distrust of the test on the part of the teachers.

Another area of concern is the manner in which we have seen test results generalized across a school system and used to stigmatize a school or even a particular teacher. If a school has an average student growth of the required 5 percent, then that school is deemed to have achieved expected student growth, but anything less tends to be viewed as a failure to attain the standard.

If, on the other hand, mean student growth rises to a higher level, the school is declared to be an Exemplary School. North Carolina also recognizes Schools of Distinction, Schools of Excellence, and Top 25 Schools. Unfortunately, there are also Low-Performing Schools.

In the case of the Exemplary School (surpassing expected student growth by the required margin), state incentive bonus money is paid. In 1996-97 it amounted to $1,000 for each certified teacher at the school. In 1997-98 the bonus was $1,500. I should add at this point that although many teachers disapprove of state testing, none to my knowledge, has refused to accept the bonus money.

Schools of Distinction are schools with 80 percent of their students on grade level. Note that with only 80 percent of students at or above grade level, a North Carolina school is considered as having achieved distinction. But remember, we are talking about student growth, and that growth establishes a standard that must be maintained. Also consider that our schools were near the bottom when national SAT scores were compared in the recent past.

This brings us to some other interesting observations. It is entirely possible to have as few as 29 percent of students on grade level and still be an Exemplary School. How can this possibly be! The answer is that the measure is student growth. The Exemplary School with only a small percentage of students on grade level must have had an even lower number at grade level the year before. And because its student test scores improved the required amount, the school qualified for both the recognition and the incentive pay. The key ingredient in this system is student growth, and growth is directly measured on student achievement tests. Are the tests important? You bet they are!

Some enlightened educators, however, have begun to view this system as a sort of pyramid scheme. In other words, can't you simply run out of room to grow? Will schools really be able to sustain these high levels of growth, and, in reality, won't they simply grow themselves off the chart?

The ABCs have two provisions to deal with this potential problem. First, there are some fancy statistical interactions in the formula that adjust for statistical regression. And secondly, a School of Distinction trumps Exemplary School. It then appears that being a School of Distinction, with 80 percent of students on or above grade level, is the way to go.

Of course, the state legislature has the authority to alter the guidelines and requirements of the ABC Plan (and in fact they have done so once already). There is already talk that the 80 percent on grade level is too low. We are expecting it to be raised, and some of us actually think that all students should be on grade level.

But what about the students who, despite our very best efforts, simply cannot achieve grade level performance on the state test? Should they be retained in that grade, and if so, for how many years? At the time of this writing, state policy makers have decided that if students in grades 3, 6, and 8 do not pass the state test, they will be retained in grade. If there is an increase in student retention of 10 percent (a not unrealistic figure as I see the situation), do we have the additional teachers and facilities to support this added effort? Many of us don't think so.

The test itself has also come under a barrage of critical fire. As addressed earlier in the chapter, North Carolina uses the multiple choice test format on end-of-grade tests. I assume this has something to do with the ease of grading these tests and, of course, these types of tests are easy targets for criticism. But in response to the apparent shortfalls of multiple choice tests, North Carolina is already planning for the day when open-ended or performance tests will be the norm.

When the 1998 test scores were released to the public this summer, the Governor stated that public schools were working in North Carolina. And those sentiments were echoed by our state school superintendent, who averred that the state's public schools had found "a formula for success."

But as many educators have come to expect, even good news can be harshly criticized. A Raleigh-based think tank recently countered the governor's optimistic view with their own report which essentially says, "All those labels are nonsense—all of N.C. schools are lousy."

Teacher Reaction

Teacher reaction to the ABC Plan has been mixed. Some teachers are never happy, disagreeing with everything. Others are easily swayed and buy into every notion and concept that comes down the pike. But most North Carolina teachers now realize that the ABCs are here to stay and that we need to embrace them and learn to function within their guidelines.

Although teacher pay in our state has been traditionally low in comparison to other states, salaries are approaching the national average early in the new century. One positive result of the ABC Plan is increased teacher salaries. But it comes at a price, because teacher pay is tied directly to student achievement.

Although most teachers are happy with the new pay scale, one colleague recently commented that she felt that her pay should be $60,000 to adequately compensate her for the added requirements imposed by the state testing program. I think she may have a point. A modest pay raise was linked to a massive increase of the demands on the teacher. We were paid more, but the demands placed on us were also significantly expanded.

In reality, teacher pay is scheduled to improve about 25 percent over four years, but one unexpected result has been to broaden the gap between teacher salaries based on years of experience. Take, for instance, a veteran teacher of 25 years. His or her expected annual salary would be $42,220 while a novice teacher with two years' experience would be paid $25,420. If the veteran teacher taught an elective course that wasn't tested at the state level, and the novice taught math, there would be an obvious inequity between teacher pay and teacher accountability.

At the end of the year the math teacher is held personally accountable for growth in student achievement; the electives teacher has no such direct accountability, although he or she would also receive incentive pay if the school qualified. The inequity of this situation is further exacerbated by the fact that the math teacher may have a class of 25 to 30 students while elective classes may contain fewer than half as many students.

Teachers are beginning to actively question the fairness of this situation. Perhaps the teacher who wants $60,000 has a point; she teaches math! Haven't we created a situation where the potential exists for an unhealthy rivalry to emerge between teachers whose students are tested, and those whose are not?

Consider the situation where Smith, a marginal tenured teacher, is viewed by his peers as an obstructionist and not a team player. He has received the $1,500 incentive pay, but his students have been undisciplined and have always entered Jones' math class in such a state of disruption that she has had to spend 15 minutes just calming them down in order to start class. According to the state plan both Smith and Jones have "earned" the bonus because their school qualified, based on student growth. But in reality, we all know that the school probably would have been able to achieve greater results had it not been for the obstructionist attitude of Smith. In addition, Jones is told to work harder to achieve School of Distinction, while Smith hopes to avoid being transferred because he wants another $1,500 next year. Is it any wonder that Jones and many of his colleagues question the fairness of this situation?

Remember, in North Carolina, bonus money is paid to each teacher at a school, not just the teachers of subjects tested under the ABC Plan. Traditionally, these monies have passed through the system into the pockets of the teachers. Now some schools have decided to spread a portion of this money among noncertified staff as well, to include custodians, office personnel, and cafeteria workers. This represents fairness at the highest level if we view a school as a community. We are all in this together and we should all share in the accrued benefit.

Administrators have their own views of the standards and accountability plan. Career administrators are in a position roughly equivalent to tenured teachers—they have job security. Nontenured administrators (tenure for new administrators was eliminated as a component of school reform) have a contract. But both groups are held accountable for student achievement and test scores. If a school fails to meet its expected growth, the administrators will be the first ones fired or transferred.

I think we could agree that administration is a challenging business these days, because principals have virtually no control over the assignment of their students and little control at best over selecting their work force. In addition, even if an administrator is willing to endure the paperwork needed to initiate the removal of a marginal or incompetent teacher, it would be difficult to find a suitable replacement in this age of teacher shortages.

The new model of shared decision making is one in which administrators and teachers are "joined at the hip," so to speak. Under the "local control" aspect of our state ABC Plan, administrators are encouraged to lead their schools in virtually any direction they see fit in order to get the job done. What is the job? Raising student test scores, of course!

One tentative conclusion can be stated here: the extra pay has been a real incentive for most teachers. Let's face it: $1,500 is a nice additional chunk of money for doing your job well. Most teachers do work extra hard to help their students achieve maximum results, and many other teachers actively support the efforts of math and language teachers.

But what will happen if we again face difficult fiscal times in our state? Will the incentive pay be withdrawn as a cost-cutting measure? There is already a rumor that the state is having difficulty funding it at current levels. I think that the withdrawal of the financial incentive would serve as a gross disincentive for continued educational reform, because so many schools have already earned incentive pay.

In addition to the performance of the overall student body, an individual teacher's performance can easily be tracked. In other words, while the principal gets an evaluation based in large part on the performance of the school, the teachers are evaluated on the performance of their students. Student test scores are beginning to be used as a direct measure of teacher performance. Is this fair? The issue certainly needs further reflection and debate.

Concluding Thoughts

From my perspective, the ABC Plan has provided many of the needed innovations to help put North Carolina's educational reform efforts on the right track for the 21st Century. Some educators have even commented that our plan is emerging as a model of effective school reform for the rest of the nation. But no matter how good a program is, there is always the potential for overreaction and abuse.

How many schools have altered their priorities from learning content to taking tests? What is really important, learning or assessment? There are so many more questions to be asked and answered.

I remember an old military adage: "Lead, Follow, or Get Out of the Way!" North Carolina's educators have a plan. It is a living document—not perfect, and not etched in stone. We all agree that reform is needed, but at least North Carolina has begun to take action. Over the next few years the ABC Plan will continue to be refined and improved upon. North Carolina educators are hopeful that some of the concerns mentioned herein will be addressed.

10

IN COLORADO, PEOPLE SHOULD ASK NOT WHAT STANDARDS CAN DO FOR THEM, BUT WHAT THEY CAN DO FOR STANDARDS

by Rob Weil

Today, more than at any time in the past, individuals and institutions associated with Colorado's public schools are feeling the pressure to change the way they do business. Reform efforts such as charter schools and vouchers are no longer subjects of educational debate. They are legislative realities. Teachers, administrators, school boards, higher education, and even community leaders are finding themselves under enormous pressure to either improve Colorado's public schools or accept these reform initiatives as a vision of Colorado's schooling future. Consequently, after years of bickering, all of these groups have found academic standards as the common ground from which to launch a concerted school improvement program. Although this new-found partnership is a welcome departure from the past, developing and implementing standards-based education is a long-term, Herculean task that will severely test the patience of this recently formed alliance. In order to fully and successfully implement Colorado's academic standards, these allies will be asked to compromise some of their deeply held—even inherent—beliefs that provide each ally with a significant level of comfort. Colorado's teachers have seen so many reform efforts fail over the past 20 years that even asking them to consider another one is unconscionable. Classroom teachers are the front-line workers who have been asked to defend all the indefensible reform efforts in the past. Plans for school improvement are usually developed far from the classroom—the educational real world. Unrealistic and unworkable initiatives are introduced at in-services and workshops for immediate implementation. Initially, teachers are publicly assured of a long-term commitment to the reform effort. Then after a year or two, the state surreptitiously moves in another direction. Teachers are left with mountains of evaluative and instructional materials that no longer reflect their district's newly adopted reform efforts. This endless cycle of adopting and discarding educational initiatives is bound to make anyone somewhat callous. It also sends a subtle but strong message to the public—schools, and the people who work in them, don't know what they are doing. This is not the message teachers want the public to receive.

School administrators have been hired with the current educational system in mind. To change the current system is to replace the same system that has afforded these people their leadership opportunities. In a sense, administrators would be cutting their own throats by championing change. To wholeheartedly embrace standards-based education would require principals and central administrators themselves to return to the classroom. Very few, if any, of Colorado's current administrators have taught in a standards-based classroom; therefore, their credibility as instructional leaders is suspect. Firsthand knowledge is crucial in helping other teachers learn the standards-based classroom. Theory of how standards work in the classroom is one thing, but there will never be a substitute for practical classroom experience.

Higher education is faced with a number of difficult issues when considering public school and academic standards. The largest and most problematic issue is admissions. If schools were to fully implement standards, colleges and universities would be asked to rethink their admissions policies. Today, higher education admissions are based primarily on a combination of grades and College Board scores. If Colorado's schools are to fully implement standards-based education, colleges and universities will need to base at least some part of their admissions on the concept of academic standards. Without this acceptance, the days of academic standards are numbered.

The community's part in academic standards is probably the greatest impediment to thoroughly and successfully implementing standards-based education. Once the process of developing academic standards is complete, the community must defend them. This means that if communities have participated fully in the development process, they have a responsibility to accept the standards as the academic mission of their schools. In other words, if a community member challenges the standards, it is the responsibility of the community—not of the teachers—to uphold the standards. In the current political climate, it's hard to believe that just such a challenge would engender a new set of academic standards or the end of academic standards altogether.

The failure of many well-meaning and sound educational reform efforts can clearly be traced to a lack of willingness on the part of one or more of the allies to leave the comfort of the existing system. Unfortunately, the implementation of academic standards in classrooms has already had a detrimental effect on classrooms across Colorado. Standards-based classrooms are characterized by the clumsiness of record-keeping and the lack of a workable vision for systemwide acceptance and adoption. This unwieldy process is jeopardizing, rather than enhancing, opportunities for student learning.

Hurdles to Academic Standards

Some of the reasons for this less than enthusiastic acceptance are clear; however, the true impediments to successful implementation of standards-based education are not so apparent. These hidden hurdles to school reform are the basic values of Colorado's educational system itself. In other words, the reason reform efforts, such as academic standards, encounter difficulties in implementation is not the concept of the reform but the set of values on which the public school system is built. Colorado's public schools were built with some very powerful core values, and many well-meaning improvement efforts are in direct conflict with them. Academic standards are no exception. Successful implementation will require Colorado's public school system not only to review its curricula and instructional practice, but also to understand the basic values on which the system stands. No reform effort can succeed without first considering the roles local control, innovation, standardized tests, forgiveness, and academic competition play in public schools.

The idea of academic standards is not new. Research has shown that virtually every other industrial country has developed a national curriculum—in a sense, national academic standards. And, if we believe all the reports, these countries' schools consistently outperform America's public schools. If these reports are legitimate, then why has the much-ballyhooed effort to implement comprehensive academic standards slowed to an imperceptible crawl? Moreover, why do teachers on the front lines of Colorado's public schools see the standards movement as dysfunctional?

The answer is much more complicated than the continually cited complaint that all meaningful public school reform is being thwarted by the oft-mentioned and never defined "education establishment." To understand the problems facing the successful implementation of any reform effort, one first must look at the underpinnings of Colorado's public school system. Clearly, many of the advocates for academic standards have aligned their work with the mission of public schools. That is simply not enough. To implement standards in public schools without considering the system's historical and contextual development will assure that standards will eventually find their way to education's already overcrowded school-improvement recycle bin.

Unfortunately, in-service programs across the state focus simply on the mechanics of implementation, which are easily replicated and should never be the reason for the success or failure of any reform effort. As almost any Colorado public school teacher can attest, the real obstacles to implementing academic standards are never addressed. Classroom teachers are assured that the philosophical conflicts between standards and the core values of public education are either being worked on at the highest levels or are not relevant. No teacher should be asked to implement any program that is so poorly developed and conceptually nebulous. The truth is that these issues must be resolved before any well-designed school improvement program can be successfully implemented and reach its full potential.

Although the following impediments to successful implementation of academic standards are not the only ones, they are among the largest. They are also among those that are never addressed in any reform effort. If anyone has ever wondered why so many educational reform efforts fail, he or she must consider whether those failed efforts have openly addressed the following core values.

Local Control

In the past, even the thought of an all-encompassing framework for curricula was seen as a threat to local control. And local control was, and still is, a sacred part of Colorado's public schools. In every school district in the state, people who represent the unique characteristics of their community are elected each year to lead the operation of the local schools. The underlying concept is that a community is above all else unique and only local people can possibly understand the educational needs of the community's children. This has been the overarching philosophy governing Colorado's schools, both public and private, since the inception of public education.

Academic standards are a direct threat to local control, plain and simple. This is why individual school districts across the state have spent enormous amounts of time and money developing their own academic standards. School boards have been reluctant to accept the state academic standards for the simple reason that what is being taught in the classroom is, and, as far as these school boards are concerned, will continue to be a local decision.

If standards are a threat to the sovereignty of local control, why in the past few years have standards become the focal point of school improvement? We would love to believe it's because of the visionary leadership of school boards across the state, with community leaders using their positions of power to lead us to the educational promised land. Unfortunately, the truth is a bit less romantic and encouraging. The standards movement is here because of political pressure. It is a compromise that all of public school's stakeholders can rally around with a minimum of organizational and constituency damage. Hence, the limited acceptance of standards. Most school districts have embraced the concept of standards as long as they are empowered to develop their own standards. In other words, districts accept the concept of academic standards but not the standardization of academics.

Standards are not a matter of geography. Standards must be universally accepted by everyone in education, both locally and beyond. To assume that your locally developed standards will match the needs of the students now and in the future is not realistic. What is worse, it's unfair. More than any time in the past, today's students will be part of a global society. For a community to handicap its students' futures because of local control over curricula is myopic and provincial.

The lack of standardization of curricula, however, is the impetus for the entire standards movement. The consistent bickering over apple and orange comparisons has made educational decisions more a matter of political persuasion than educational appropriateness. Implementing academic standards was heralded as the educational reform that would end these controversial comparisons and establish a level playing field that would enable all schools to make data-based educational decisions. Most importantly, these results could be replicated in other schools because of the standardization of academics.

Many educational leaders will openly argue that the standardization of curricula is not the reason for the academic standards movement. Standards are an effort to raise the academic bar within the system. Ultimately, standards are a way of bringing more accountability to the classroom. Although these arguments make sense and are politically powerful, they tend to intensify one of education's largest problems—the blanket acceptance of subjectivity in a context of objectivity. One of the most difficult issues when dealing with accountability in the classroom is that of objectivity. Every teacher has a unique professional context, different students with different abilities, and a wide range of available resources. All of these factors play a significant role in the success of each and every classroom. Systems of instructional accountability are continually developed that discount or only lightly touch on these crucial factors. Without serious consideration of these issues, however, accountability will continue to be a major point of contention and will impede the successful implementation of academic standards.

For instructional accountability to be embraced within Colorado's public school system, academic standards must be seen as all-encompassing. Teachers must feel that they are being held to basically the same instructional standards as their peers statewide and nationwide. Instructional accountability cannot occur just on a local level, but on a wider level as well. All teachers know that their district test scores are compared nationally. Doesn't it follow that their instructional practice should also be? But this can only be done when what one teacher is asked to accomplish is similar to what another is expected to accomplish. If accountability is an ultimate goal, then academic standards must be uniform if not universal.

The role of local control must be openly discussed if academic standards are to reach their full potential. To either deny that the conflict exists or to avoid the question altogether is to ensure the ultimate failure of the standards effort. Local control has always formed the backbone of the American educational system, but perhaps the implementation of standards has exposed the limitations and biases of local school boards. Such a revelation challenges the basic structure of Colorado's public schools—not to mention the venerated tradition of local control.

Standardized Tests and Their Impact

The chicken-or-egg problem in public schools is how to ensure that teachers do not teach to the test while at the same time using tests as the most definitive measure of performance. Every teacher in the state has struggled with the ideal that improved test results should somehow be an indirect result of improved classroom instruction. Virtually every other business solves its most critical problems by addressing them directly. This is not the case with education in Colorado. Although we do acknowledge the role test scores play in the evaluation of school performance, we assert that test scores alone do not fully represent a school's overall performance. The concept that test scores are not the sole measure of schools, however, is questioned every time the scores are published in the local newspapers.

Teachers are always cautioned about "teaching to the test." Such an act is construed as the ultimate educational sin. What is ironic—maybe the more apt word is "moronic"—about indicting teachers for teaching to the test is that teaching to the test is what is expected of good teachers every day. No teacher would test students on material that he or she did not cover in class. If teachers did, they should expect phone calls from parents, student complaints, and administrative reprimands. At the very least, a teacher who routinely evaluated students on material not taught would lose instructional credibility. What does this paradox say about our educational system? The answer is far worse than the question.

By avoiding the transgression of teaching to the test, we have created a system that requires increased test results to be accidental. Clearly, test results are only part of a holistic assessment. Although this is a concept no sound educator would question, the reality is that standardized test results, right or wrong, are used as the number one indicator of a school's or district's performance. They are used every day to compare and contrast schools and even evaluate an entire country's schooling system. The simple fact is that the public will always use standardized test scores as the deciding factor in performance.

In every classroom in the state, accountability for the standardized test scores is undeniable. Teachers, principals, superintendents, and the community clearly understand the importance of students doing well on any standardized assessment. Then why do they lose sight of this reality as they develop standards? Districts and schools identify their own academic standards without proper consideration of the impact of those standards on the students' test scores. Standards are developed in committee rooms where individual bias plays a larger role than does consideration of the eventual performance assessment.

Academic standards and their assessments will never replace standardized test assessment. Student performance on standardized tests was the reason schools were asked to change originally. To dismiss the importance the public places on these test results is to avoid the reason there was such a powerful call for school reform in the first place. The public wasn't demanding school reform because the assessments were flawed; the public was decrying the poor performance of the students on those assessments. So why are we developing an entirely new academic system, with new assessments, if schools have not focused instruction on the one assessment that has national validity—standardized test scores? Again, the answer is in the underlying values of Colorado's public education.

Infatuation with Innovation

One of Colorado's public schools' most powerful core values is innovation. When there is a problem in schools today, we don't remediate, we innovate. Innovation can be a positive influence when it is placed in the proper context. More times than not, however, the drive for innovation in schools becomes obsessive. Schools compete, not on student performance, but on innovation. This is a major mistake. Educators have accepted the premise that the most innovative school will also be the most successful. That is clearly not the case.

The importance of innovation in schools is evident in all major educational publications. Each one is filled with new ways to schedule, instruct, and assess. Innovation can be positive when it is used to enhance student achievement, but "new-and-different" has become an end in itself.

Innovation can be found as the impetus for almost every school improvement program. Although improving student performance is the ostensible goal of every reform effort, accolades are invariably accorded to educational innovation. This is why teachers face the nightmare of a dual system of academic standards and grades in virtually every classroom struggling to implement standards-based education in Colorado. The sheer denial of the schools' obsession with innovation is, in itself, a major problem.

Anyone who has taught a class in the past few years can attest to the influence of educational innovation in the classroom. Teachers are being evaluated not on their skills as teachers but on their ability to innovate. What makes this reality so discouraging is that many administrators don't believe there is a difference. Moreover, many educational leaders confuse innovation with the technique of adjusting instruction to meet the needs of a student and, because of the obsession with innovation, ask teachers to individualize for every student.

Teachers are often criticized when the lessons they are using are not original or informed by the latest educational thought. Although those lessons may have been proven educationally sound and have been performance-tested, evaluators are still looking for innovation. Even a cursory look at a standardized test and the area being tested, however, will show that test content is not innovative. In fact, standardized means something established by general conformity, whereas innovation demands novelty and unusualness. We don't necessarily want students who come up with unusual answers to math problems or punctuation. We want students who get it right.

Teachers clearly would value the chance to exchange instructional ideas with their colleagues; this does happen on a limited basis. The sharing of ideas, however, does not parallel public schools' preoccupation with innovation; therefore, the open exchange of instructional practice is only informally supported. This is the reason why so many teachers struggle with the implementation of standards-based education. School districts provide very little in the way of lessons or assessments for academic standards simply because teachers are to be, above all else, innovative.

Accepting the concept that innovation is a value that must never be limited is a serious mistake that most schools make. Without control, innovation has a way of overpowering even the best of schools. It is intoxicating and invigorating, but it is not necessarily the answer to improving performance. Innovation clearly has a place in schools; however, it can never have a primary role in a system developed to give citizens a common ground for exchanging and developing ideas and knowledge.

Forgiveness

The Colorado public school system is based on forgiveness, plain and simple. Students face no real consequences for academic failure until they reach high school. Most schools move children through the system based solely on age. Even if students fall behind their peers, more than likely they will not be held back. They may be placed in extra instructional programs that remediate their deficiencies. Eventually, at some point, they are required to accumulate credits for graduation. Many would argue, however, that even requiring a student to accumulate credits in high school doesn't ensure the student has learned anything. This is not a flaw in the system, but rather, the effect of forgiveness shaping our schools.

Forgiveness in public schools is a reflection of the society in which schools exist. The prevailing theme of Colorado's schools is that anyone can shed the mistakes of the past and use the educational system to turn his or her life around. America is full of people who either made mistakes or were the victims of unfortunate circumstances and then used the educational system to achieve great things. These success stories come with a price. In order for people to use education to turn their lives around, they first must fall through the cracks in the system.

This is not to say that the system fails people on purpose. Quite the contrary: it is built on the American value of hard work. If students work hard, they will learn. Moreover, if a student didn't work hard at first, he or she can always begin to work hard and achieve. This is the concept of forgiveness that underpins the American public school system. Even though other countries have severe consequences for failure in school at an early age, that is their society's way, not ours. When we consider any reform effort such as standards, we must align it with the concept of forgiveness.

Forgiveness, however, can be one of the most troubling aspects of academic standards. How do we hold students accountable for performance while assuring that the schools do not abandon forgiveness? The question, "What happens when a student doesn't meet the standard?" has been asked a million times. There is no clear, concise answer because of the natural conflict between the concept of forgiveness and academic standards. This dichotomy is no small problem. The whole future of academic standards will be determined by the answer.

Many educators respond to this dichotomy by favoring forgiveness. Students who fail to meet academic standards will be given extra help to "catch up" with their peers. How is this different from what we now have? Students who fall behind their peers on our current assessments receive extra instructional support to catch up. The belief that remediating to meet an academic standard is inherently different from and ultimately better than the extra help students receive now is absurd. Whether remediating to meet an academic standard or any other curricular concept is not the point. What all schools must deal with when implementing any new reform effort is that forgiveness is intrinsic in American schools.

Forgiveness is the core value that most clearly sets us apart from other school systems around the world. To successfully implement a standards-based education system would require that the forgiveness concept so pervasive in public schools be presently addressed. Asking teachers to implement a program that has very few workable answers to the question of what happens when a student fails to meet the standard is only going to ensure substandard success.

Student Competition

The advocates of standards-based education have articulated the belief that academic standards are ultimately superior to the archaic letter grade system now used in public schools. Standards will clearly define what students are to know and when they are to know it. Additionally, parents will know what their child is learning and how proficient he or she is in relation to specific academic criteria. Letter grades will still be given as in the past, but the standards report will be the true reflection of progress. Without a doubt, standards can help increase student achievement, but this issue is not just a matter of mechanics. Instead, it is a matter of accountability and, most importantly, competition.

Academic competition is as much a part of America's public schools as yellow buses. Schools are based on the idea of competition both inside and out. Internally, schools use letter grades and standardized tests to select and sort students. Since the inception of public schools, there have been valedictorians and "tail-end Charlies." Today, as part of the forgiving nature of schools, we don't publicly recognize the less able students, but they still exist. Externally, schools and districts are driven to compete with neighboring districts or other schools. Urban schools are compared to suburban schools that, in turn, are compared to private schools. Recently, charter schools, vouchers, and for-profit schools have increased the stakes. Colorado's public schools are facing more external competition now than ever in the past. Some educators unfortunately mistake support for public schools as opposition to the idea of competition between schools. This is not the case, however. Most of the support for public schools is a belief in the idea of fair play when schools are asked to compete. Public schools should be allowed to compete on a level playing field in regard to funding and other socioeconomic factors.

To believe that the public wants a parallel assessment system that simply creates check-off lists for learning is missing the reason for all the criticism of public schools in the first place. The reason for the focus on school reform was that, all across America, schools were not seen as being competitive with their counterparts from other nations. In Colorado, standardized test scores in both high school and grade school slowly decreased. This trend added even more fuel to the reform fire. These two perceptions are the primary reason public schools are under so much pressure to change. It's not just that Colorado's schools are not seen as good; it's that they are not seen to be as competitive as they need to be.

Most recent implementations of academic standards do not directly address the issue of competition. Reporting that a student is proficient on a standard does not indicate how the student will fare when he or she competes for a job, a scholarship, or admission to college. Any new reform effort must directly and convincingly increase and convey to the public the competitiveness of schools. A number of school reform efforts have increased communication between school and home. If standards-based education is going to succeed, however, it must communicate the message that Colorado's public schools are more competitive than ever before.

The Successful Implementation of Standards

For academic standards to be successfully implemented and make Colorado's public schools better, all people and institutions associated with them must be willing to rethink their role in schools. Teachers, administrators, school boards, higher education, and the community must all address the five hurdles to academic standards. These impediments have been avoided for much too long because of the anxiety they cause. Local control, the role of standardized tests, innovation, forgiveness, and competition are clearly in the way of successfully implementing academic standards. Schools, and the people who work within them, can no longer act as if these hurdles don't exist or that standards can work in concert with them. That's not the case. Unless we acknowledge them, we will have to face the unpleasant results of ignoring them. There are no easy answers to complex problems, and this is no exception. The future of public schools is in question.

Dealing with Local Control

As noted previously, local control is a core value from which Colorado's public schools operate. In the past, school districts were isolated and only had to reflect the values of the local community. With all the advances in communications, the world has become a smaller place. A student from a small local community is more of a world citizen than ever before. And because of this, we must run our school districts less like kingdoms and more as part of a larger academic system. If we ever want our students to compete on a worldwide scale, our schools must prepare them and assess them according to national and international standards.

To compete on a worldwide scale, school districts must develop curricula with a global perspective. This doesn't mean that American history or other similar subjects are removed from the curriculum; it simply means that where appropriate, academic standards should parallel the curricula of other countries. If we want our students to compete with students from other countries, we must provide them with equal opportunities. Such a position does not advocate a national curriculum, but it is premised on the basic belief that academic standards should be standardized. If every district in the state adopts its own academic standards, where is the standardization? The implementation of academic standards will have accomplished nothing. Every time a comparison of student performance is made, the same old concerns about comparing apples and oranges will start. The only way to honestly compare student achievement is to start with the same basic academic standards.

In order for academic standards to make public schools more accountable, all local school boards need to reconsider their own development of academic standards. If the state's standards are not considered rigorous enough, then it is incumbent upon the local school boards to require that the state raise the level of its standards. Once the standards are agreed upon and standardized, then, and only then, can public schools be held accountable.

Colorado's public schools are some of the most political institutions in the state, and academic standards are unfortunately not immune to the vagaries of politics. The state board of education should set academic standards and stand by them. To allow local boards of education to review, rewrite, or delete all or any part of the state's standards is simply a way to allow those who demand public school accountability to avoid accountability themselves. If the targets public schools are trying to hit are continually shifting, assuredly a number of public schools will spend their resources aiming in the wrong direction.

The constituents within local school districts should spend their limited time not only on a curriculum with a global perspective, but also on how this curriculum is taught. In order to do this, each group must first accept its responsibility for how things are taught. Teachers should spend their planning time sharing ideas and learning from others in order to refine their lessons. School boards and administrators must see themselves as providers of support and spend their time supplying more of the resources teachers need to be successful. They should focus on increasing planning time, instructional materials, and staff development opportunities that allow teachers to share successful instructional strategies with each other. This is the only way that the accountability that so many people want in public schools has a chance.

School boards correctly believe that academic requirements are specific to their community, but they must acknowledge that their community is the world. This concept is a monumental leap from where we are today. Just starting with meaningful, accepted state academic standards would be the first positive step in making standards a school improvement idea that actually makes a difference.

Bring on the Standardized Tests

Standardized tests are here to stay. It's time for all public schools and their constituents to deal with them directly and openly. As long as schools continue to characterize some standardized test results as invalid or only a partial indication of achievement, the public will continue to perceive that schools are trying to somehow cover up their inability to teach. Recently, some public schools have spent time helping their students with test-taking preparations. This is a teaching-to-the-test approach without teaching what's on the test. These preparations have increased the school's overall performance on the tests, but a new approach is the only thing that will truly place standardized tests in the proper perspective.

Public schools must be willing to show the public that no matter what assessment is used, students who attend school and work hard can do well. In order to do this, schools must be willing to open up and accept a new standardized test philosophy that hasn't been very popular in the past. Instead of ambiguously teaching to the test, schools must test what is taught. The concept of test congruency is the nemesis of all teachers faced with standardized testing. On some standardized assessments, teachers are left guessing what is on the test. This sounds like an elementary concept, but the test congruency of a number of national standardized tests is never questioned. In other words, if the district is asking teachers to teach locally developed standards and their students are going to take either a national or state assessment, teachers should demand that the test directly assess those specific standards. Moreover, if the national or state standardized test does not directly reflect the district's academic standards, why is the district using it? Scoring well on any assessment should never be left to chance. If academic standards are going to drive a district's curriculum, then every assessment must be an indicator of performance in relation to those local standards. It is inherently unfair to hold teachers accountable for an assessment that is not directly derived from the standards they are required to teach. This means one of two things must happen, both of which are almost unheard of in public schools. A district either must use only standardized assessments developed entirely from its own academic standards or it must develop local standards based entirely upon the national or state assessments.

These two options are the only way to ensure that the standardized test results released every year to the public are truly reflective of what teachers are being asked to teach. Many of the advocates for academic standards correctly state that standardized test results will never completely represent a student's learning. To talk of portfolios or other cleverly named bodies of evidence as further indicators of a student's progress is to obfuscate the point of public school improvement. The call for school reform was not based on the belief that teachers didn't have enough evidence of a student's learning: it was based on a perception that student achievement was decreasing because standardized test scores were falling. Unless the advocates for these additional testaments to student achievement do a tremendous amount of public relations in the very near future, the chances that the public at large will accept them as readily as they do test scores, is quite remote.

Educational Innovation

Innovation has a role in education. It is important for teachers to improve their lessons for the sake of measurable learning. Reflective innovation in concert with instructional review and student assessment is an important part of improving teaching practice. To say that innovation is not part of school improvement is foolish; however, that part must be tempered with a continuous focus on the reasons schools exist and the aims of education. Schools exist to ensure that society has an informed and educated citizenry. An innovation should only be brought into the schools when it can measurably increase the success of this mission. Too many times innovative programs are implemented because of the pressure to change, rather than the need to improve performance.

To innovate for the sake of change is wrong. Many of the innovative programs that are started in schools are unable to show demonstrable improvement in student performance. They are implemented simply for effect. They misguidedly address the public's demand for increased student performance. What is worse, once these programs are up and running, they become institutionalized. In Colorado, many innovative programs were begun in the belief that they would improve student performance. Today, these programs are used more for public relations than meaningful school reform. The basic problem with educational innovation is an unwillingness of the advocates of innovation to accept the same measure of accountability for themselves that they demand from others.

Academic standards are the next innovation that has the potential to fail not because of the concept, but because of the difficulties of implementing it correctly. Teachers across Colorado are being asked to implement an entirely new system of assessment and instruction without a commensurate amount of planning time. Systems of assessment require that teachers relinquish inordinate amounts of instructional time just to meet the minimum requirements of the implementation. The amount of record keeping that academic standards require makes the entire system virtually unworkable. Additionally, the public is being assured that the traditional grades and standardized tests will not suffer and will remain a focus of school improvement. This acceptance of a dual system of assessment is innovation at its worst.

Academic standards need to be implemented not as innovation, but as a logical method of addressing the public's concern about student performance. This can only happen if standards directly address the assessments the public wants. Developing a new system of assessment is just educational innovation running amok.

The Idea of Forgiveness and Standards

Public schools have grown to accept the core value of forgiveness, but when it comes to academic standards, we need an exception to forgiveness. For standards to succeed, everyone must be accountable, and most particularly, the student. Students need to understand that academic standards are "where the rubber hits the road." They are the definitive measurement of the skills a student has acquired at this point in time.

Holding students accountable for their own learning is an important step in making academic standards a school reform that works. The idea that students are passive victims of education is one of the most ominous factors that classroom teachers face today. Of course, teachers should be accountable for the learning that goes on in their classrooms, but for accountability to work, it must be a two-way street. A perfect example of the effect of holding students accountable can be found in the state's driver's exam. All students clearly know the consequences of failing their driver's test: they don't get to drive. Any high school teacher can tell you that very few students fail their driving test. That is the effect of setting standards and holding learners accountable.

Many educators worry that holding the students accountable for meeting the rigorous academic standards will cause some students to feel inferior or incapable of meeting such requirements. To a small extent, there are students who will have to struggle to successfully achieve some of the more challenging concepts. As shown by the driver's test, however, students can easily recognize the standards and the rewards or consequences of meeting or failing to meet them. Students develop a sense of self-worth when they know that what they have accomplished is a worthwhile task. Students also know what is required of them if they fail to accomplish it—that is, unless well-meaning educators confuse them by not holding them accountable.

Although forgiveness and successfully implementing a system of academic standards are mutually exclusive concepts, each has its place in public education. The key is in forgiving students for not passing a standard requirement and providing them with remediation, but not allowing them to slip through on social promotion.

Competition Has a Place

Colorado's public schools are like all schools across the country; they have a duty to help students discover their strengths and weaknesses. This natural selection is as important a part of a student's education as the academics themselves. Academic competition is the cornerstone of this process. Standards are based on the belief that all students can learn. The problem is that not all students learn in the same way or at the same rate. That's where academic standards become complicated. Standards must count, and, in order for them to count, students must demonstrate their learning.

Higher education uses academic competition as a way to sort and then select their students. For academic standards to have any chance of becoming a reality, America's most prestigious colleges and universities must include standards and assessments as part of the requirements for admission. Colleges would only accept standards as an integral part of admission if they were somehow standardized. Local control makes this almost impossible. It's no big secret that College Board exams are important because they are a way for colleges to compare students' academic ability on the same assessment at the same time in the students' lives. This is competition in its purest form.

For standards to be successful, they must fit into the competitive environment of college admissions without adding to concern over unequal educational opportunities. Colleges, universities, junior colleges, and all the other postsecondary institutions are major customers of the public schools. And as customers, they will compare students based on the most objective criteria available. Standards will only succeed if they are secure and have an ability to differentiate students through valid and reliable assessments. In a sense, this is the concept of fair play when it comes to academic competition. If standards are not uniform across the country, they will only exacerbate the problem of unequal educational opportunity.

What We Can Do for Standards

For standards to improve student performance there must be a willingness on the part of everyone associated with Colorado's public schools to rethink their roles. Successful implementation of academic standards will require everyone from the state legislature to the classroom teacher to agree on one of two unpopular alternatives. Public schools can accept a new set of guiding principles or realize that academic standards must be redeveloped with the core values of Colorado's public schools openly addressed and incorporated. The most desirable and realistic choice is to refocus standards by adjusting the current core values of the public schools. This would be a real step forward for Colorado's public schools. Many people who have significant influence in Colorado's educational circles, however, would prefer to see the entire public school system reworked. The inability to agree on a single overarching philosophical approach to education is one of the reasons public schools have struggled for so long. Moreover, it is the reason academic standards are an implementation nightmare for Colorado's classroom teachers.

For current versions of academic standards to be successfully implemented, all involved—from classroom teachers to the community—must accept a revised set of core values in schools. The guiding principles that created Colorado's school system have become obstacles that hinder reform efforts, such as academic standards, from reaching their full potential. Values such as local control, the role of standardized tests, innovation, forgiveness, and academic competition must be reevaluated and reformed if academic standards are to become the touchstones of education in Colorado in the twenty-first century.

11

TEACHERS' PERSPECTIVES: A COLLEAGUE'S COMMENTARY

by Jean Fontana

One glaring generalization that can be made based on the information provided by the teacher authors of this book is that teachers support the standards movement. We also know that our students can successfully meet demanding standards, provided they persevere. Standards are just the latest featured promontory on the educational landscape, like all those recently "nationalized" countries on an old map of the USSR—always been there but unrecognized by most. And like those struggling nations, American teachers in trying to implement this latest initiative just continue to cope with some of the same operating insanities: no money, no resources, no input, no status. In fact, our capacity for coping is so pervasive that those who perceive themselves as true bolsheviks of educational reform are dismayed with teachers' willingness to embrace the standards movement.

But look at it from our perspective. We are herded in so many different and sometimes dangerous directions by these same snapping dogs that when we see a path that is relatively benign we acquiesce. Like the parents of teenagers, we have learned to pick our fights. And there isn't anything inherently evil in upholding standards, provided they are clear, achievable, and worthy of the effort.

Although teachers accept standards, we do vary in our attitudes as to what they will be able to accomplish. Some teachers adopt their accompanying conceptual buzz-words with great hope. These are usually the teachers who have been involved in the grass-roots efforts that resulted in their development. I was involved in a similar effort when the Degrees of Reading Power test was first brought into my district by the College Board. Along with a few administrators, teachers became members of a closely knit cadre involved with instructional design. We still share a strong bond long after the group's dissolution. (This is perhaps the most powerful way of bringing about institutional change, but it never seems to be given enough time or funding to take hold.)

Other teachers, while willing to give standards a try, are more pessimistic. Some are waiting for the promised perks of this most recent reform effort to materialize. A few are just biding their time, picking and choosing what they like, while waiting for this newest onslaught to just fade away, as have the reform efforts of the past.

This range of attitudes is also remarkable in view of all the attempts to homogenize us. Homogenization always seems to be the desired outcome when dealing with teachers. Just think of all those teacher-proof manuals and programs, textbook-centered curricula, and method-implicit lessons. Forget about artistry. Novice teachers are told about the seven ways to increase motivation, the six characteristics of an effective example, and the five characteristics of retention. Participants are also given a laundry list of things to do during the presentation of a stand-up lesson (such as move about the room) and are then cautioned by the college professor who is glued to the podium, "Above all don't lecture, be innovative." The teacher's edition of the spelling text lists the precise way we all are to administer a test: say the spelling word; use it in a sentence; say it again. Does anyone anywhere do it differently?

And it's getting worse. Recently principals at ASCD's Urban Professional Development Institute were told that they should require teachers to list on the board each day three things for students to read as they enter the classroom: homework assignments; busy work (euphemistically called "warm-up activities"); and the learning objective for the lesson (Checkley, 1999). This teacher-management technique is called "blackboard configuration," and its proponents at the School Leadership Academy claim that it will not only help teachers stay on task but will also make daily observations meaningful. Meaningful for whom? So much for all these new ideas about teacher development. Is it any wonder that so many bright aspiring teachers go into other fields?

Those of us who have heard these messages of homogenization but still continue to teach have discovered that our painfully acquired coping abilities combined with sick humor help us deal with such idiocy. And it's a good thing, because educational idiocy seems to be bi-coastal. From sea to shining sea, uninterrupted teaching time is scarce. Is Japan the only place where PA announcements don't interrupt lessons?

Teachers in Los Angeles resent not having telephones and other technology, just as much as Long Island teachers do. And teachers in both the North and the South bristle when they hear such acronyms as IEP and ADHD.

The paltry amount that North Carolina teachers receive as merit pay gets this Yankee's blood boiling.

Regardless of their location, teachers expect their students to learn. We're not willing to accept less from them. When we make up and administer our own tests and assessments, we expect every student to pass. We don't think of bell-shaped results. We get downright annoyed when our students don't achieve mastery. We also expect everyone else around us to be functioning at the same high-performance level, and therein lies the problem.

But teachers are also a forgiving lot. Forgiveness, as Weil points out, is truly a core value of our educational system. Maybe it shouldn't be. American teachers are constantly being told that our entire system of education must be more like those of nations whose students score higher on the TIMSS (Third International Mathematics and Science Study) test. This American teacher has never seen a TIMSS test, nor do I personally know of any student who has taken this test, although our superintendent believes that some of our students have taken it. And I'm from New York, the testing capital of the nation. Whom do I forgive for this?

Recently, teachers in my district elected and then actively supported the reelection of a legislator whose parent had been a member of our board of education during one of the longest teacher strikes in the history of New York. Teachers were not going to let the "sins of the parent" be visited upon the child. How could we? We were thanked for our New York liberal open-mindedness by the passage of charter school legislation. Will our union forgive all the legislators who voted for this bill because it was tied directly to pay raises for the legislature?

Another generalization that can be gleaned from our chapter authors is the need for conversations. Nobody seems to talk to teachers. Oh, teachers dialogue with students and engage in questions and answers, but that kind of repartee centers around subject matter or student-centered concerns. While sometimes enlightening, parent-teacher discourse is often one-sided. At meetings and in-service courses teachers are talked at. No wonder we eagerly engage in conversations with strangers on airplanes, knowing full well what the upshot of such discourse will be. Sidney Rauch, a professor of reading instruction at Hofstra University, often spoke in class about conversations he had on planes, which he described as "reading diagnosis at 30,000 feet."

Evidently no one talks to teachers in higher ed either. Let's start having conversations—real conversations like the ones teachers have in school corridors. Higher education faculty should drop into the faculty or copier room when observing their student teachers. If you talk to—not at—us, we'll talk to you. I promise. It could be an informative part of your day; it certainly will be a highlight of ours. You can't believe how such visits improve the climate of the school, but it is often a lost opportunity for mutual learning. Why, we'd even welcome sit-down discussions with some administrators from central office or state ed. Those once a year walks-through-the-school-building don't do anything for us.

Schiller says, ". . . if you take a rich chunk of classroom practice and shake it, standards and benchmarks fall out." If only those were the ones that everyone else could see, we wouldn't be arguing over whose standards we should use. If you take that same rich chunk and examine it you'll also find the appropriate mix that assessment should play. Diagnosing strengths and weaknesses through formative types of assessment helps teachers recognize the kind of instruction that their students need. But it is instruction through meaningful experiences and activities that results in learning.

As Hogan reminds us, teachers want to make a difference in the life of a child. We did not become teachers because we wanted to raise test scores. But we want to have a place at the table where standards, tests, and accountability are being discussed. We'll bring along our own unique views, and we won't hold it against anyone that the invitation came at the last minute. We're used to being completely ignored. And that has been a fatal mistake!

References

Checkley, K. 1999. Order in the classroom: A disciplined approach to teacher observations. *ASCD Education Update,* 41, March: 5.

12

STANDARDS, TESTS, AND ACCOUNTABILITY: WHAT THEY MEAN FOR THE CLASSROOM TEACHER

by Allan A. Glatthorn

The purpose of this concluding chapter is to offer some suggestions for the classroom teachers who have to deal with standards, tests, and accountability. The suggestions that follow are based on three sources: what the teacher-authors of this book have written; what this author has learned by teaching students and talking with teachers; and what researchers have discovered.

Coping with Standards

Unlike most educational innovations, standards are here to stay. As Fontana notes, they have been with us in different guises for many years. And the continuing pressure for better student achievement will likely sustain them for many years to come. So what are teachers to do? The answer given here and in previous chapters is simple: cope. Teachers can cope in many effective ways, as follows:

- Analyze the high stakes tests to determine which standards and their related benchmarks are likely to be tested. Not all standards and benchmarks will be tested. Here are two examples from the Kendall/Marzano (1997) compilation of benchmarks for fifth-and sixth-grade United States history.

- Understands that "chance events" had an impact on history. (p. 113)

- Understands peaceful and conflictory interaction between English settlers and Native Americans... (p. 136)

The first benchmark is not likely to be tested; the second probably will be. I call the unlikely-to-be tested the *enrichment benchmarks*; the likely-to-be-tested, the *mastery benchmarks*.

- By reviewing your texts, reflecting about your students, and analyzing the tests, decide which mastery units you can adapt or develop. You can adapt old units that you have successfully taught before and develop new ones that fill the gap. The mastery units will incorporate the mastery benchmarks, relating them to more general themes or concepts.

• Build a yearly (or semester) schedule, listing the titles of the mastery units and indicating how much time they will take. Some experts recommend that the mastery-based units should altogether take no more than 70 per cent of available time. This allocation accommodates the usual slippages in school life and also gives you time for enrichment, review, and remediation.

• Also note in the calendar the sequence of all the units, being sure that the mastery units are studied before the tests are administered.

You can enter all this information into a form like the one shown in Figure 12.1. A portion of the form has been filled in, to illustrate how it might be used. The complete form would list all the weeks of the school year, in sequence. It would also note any events (national, local, or school) that would affect teaching and learning. The third column would note the titles of units; the last, the type—mastery or enrichment.

FIGURE 12.1
Sample Yearly Calendar

Weeks	Major Events	Unit Titles	Unit Type
9/2-9/13	Parents Night	War or Peace? Relations with Native Americans	Mastery
5/1-5	Talent Show	Your and Your Family's Past	Enrichment

The main point here is to use the standards and their benchmarks as a way to systematize and focus your teaching and planning. You can develop effective units that are both standards-based and student-sensitive.

As several of the authors have noted, these processes will take time and need to be accompanied by effective staff development. The staff development should take the form of teaching teams working together during quality time, exchanging ideas, sharing materials, and generally learning together.

Coping with High-Stakes Tests

High-stakes tests (those the results of which are used for making decisions about summer school, graduation, retention, and teacher performance) also seem like a predictable part of teachers' future. The authors of these chapters have noted several problems with such tests:

- The tests do not match the standards or what teachers consider important.

- The administration of such tests is often messy and error-filled.

- They take time away from teaching.

- They are expensive to administer and score.

- The scoring is slow and often flawed.

- They often push educators to act unethically.

In support of this last conclusion, teachers reported that approximately 22 percent of their colleagues either often or frequently "provided hints on correct answers"; about 20 percent were reported as often or frequently giving more time to students than the directions indicated (Shepard and Dougherty, 1991).

As a response to such criticisms, some states are moving towards "performance tests," which require students to solve complex open-ended problems and to demonstrate their knowledge and skills. Such performances and demonstrations, however, have their own problems: they are very difficult to score validly and reliably; and administering and scoring such tests are even more time-consuming and expensive.

So how can teachers cope with both types of tests—and do so in an ethical manner? As explained above, you can analyze their content to develop mastery units; obviously you should do so by using only nonconfidential materials. If you build effective mastery units, your students should perform well without experiencing day after day of drill and practice. This observation is supported by some research indicating that students who experienced lessons emphasizing critical thinking and problem solving did just as well as those who had only drill and practice on test-like items.

It also makes sense to develop "test wiseness" in students. Focused units on test-taking skills should be taught just before the tests are to be given, so that the skills are fresh in mind at test time. Besides teaching test-taking skills, teachers should also stress the importance of the tests—for the student, the teacher, the parents, and the school. Several anecdotal reports from teachers indicate that students often do not take such tests seriously.

Can your students get good results on state tests without your focusing on test-like items and using every class for drill and practice? The answer from the foregoing chapters and the empirical research is clearly "yes."

Coping with Teacher Accountability

The third issue highlighted by these authors is teacher accountability. As the term is generally used, it is a system that operates from the following beliefs:

- Teachers are the only ones responsible for their students' achievement.

- The best measure of students' achievement is their performance on state-mandated high-stakes tests.

- The state and the school district should reward teachers whose students get high scores and punish those whose students do poorly.

All these beliefs are challenged by research findings.

- Several factors beyond the control of the classroom teacher affect student achievement: peer influence; parent involvement in and cooperation with the school; the way time is used outside of school (doing homework or watching television); school climate; student motivation; student age. (See Fraser, et al, 1987.)

- The most important outcomes of education go beyond what traditional tests can measure. Consider these outcomes—all of which are rarely measured: develop and act upon ethical standards; enjoy reading poetry; value mathematics as a way of knowing; develop scientific curiosity. Most standardized tests measure only low-level knowledge and comprehension skills. Even the more valid performance assessments have their own faults: too time-consuming to administer; too difficult to score objectively and reliably; and too expensive to use on a state-wide basis.

- Teachers are motivated chiefly by intrinsic rewards, the satisfaction that comes from seeing students grow.

Despite this lack of research support, teachers are being held accountable. Besides taking the political action discussed below, there are some practical steps that teachers can take.

One useful response to externally imposed accountability systems that are not supported by sound research is for teachers and school administrators to work together to develop internal accountability systems. An internal accountability system is one in which all those inside the school who are involved directly or indirectly in students' learning are held accountable to each other. Figure 12.2 shows the complexity of such a system. There is some early evidence that schools with internal accountability systems are more capable than those with externally developed systems.

To understand the specific nature of teacher accountability as one aspect of such a complex system, consider the "I am accountable" statements shown in Figure 12.3. They are presented here only as an illustration of an effective and equitable teacher accountability system.

In addition to that positive response, teachers should keep in mind the following professional commitments:

- Teach as best as you can.

- Continue to develop professionally.

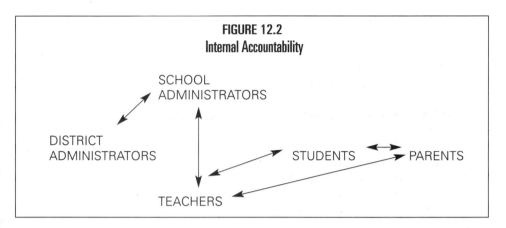

FIGURE 12.2
Internal Accountability

SCHOOL ADMINISTRATORS

DISTRICT ADMINISTRATORS

STUDENTS ⟷ PARENTS

TEACHERS

FIGURE 12.3
Teacher Accountability

I am accountable to parents to...
1. Welcome their involvement and cooperation.
2. Keep them informed.
3. Seek their input about helping their son or daughter.
4. Help them implement a learning-centered home environment.

I am accountable to school and district administrators to...

1. Implement district policies.
2. Teach as best I can.
3. Implement the district curriculum.
4. Continue my professional development, welcoming all attempts to help me grow.
5. Act ethically and morally.

I am accountable to students to...

1. Help them learn, to the extent of my ability.
2. Evaluate their progress, keeping them and their parents fully informed.
3. Believe in them and their potential.
4. Help them connect with the curriculum.
5. See them as individuals, avoiding ethnic stereotypes.
6. Provide a learning-centered classroom environment.
7. Help them develop the motivation to learn.

- Carry out your own classroom research on these issues, as they affect your teaching and student learning.

- When problems develop, solve them and avoid blaming. Learning problems are caused by a multiplicity of factors—and usually can be solved through joint efforts. Blaming students, parents, or administrators does no good.

Taking Political Action

Standards, tests, and accountability systems are here to stay—for a long while, probably. But through concerted political action, they can be—and need to be—changed. Instead of docilely accepting these mechanisms as necessary evils, teachers should work through their local, state, and national professional associations to change these dysfunctional policies.

References

Fraser, J., H. H. Walberg, W. W. Welch, and J. A. Hattie 1987. Syntheses of educational productivity research. *International Journal of Education*, 11: 73-145.

Kendall, J. S., and R. J. Marzano. 1997. *Content knowledge*. Alexandria, Va.: Association for Supervision and Curriculum Development.

Shepard, L. A., and K. C. Dougherty. 1991. *Effects of high stakes testing on instruction*. Paper presented at annual meeting of the American Educational Research Association, April. Chicago.

ABOUT THE AUTHORS

Katherine Bauer-Sanders is a program coordinator and bilingual teacher for an educational readiness project on a Winnebago reservation. An experienced preschool and kindergarten teacher and a reading specialist, she has recently organized a no-cost reading clinic for struggling readers in her community. She is completing her doctorate at the University of South Dakota.

Jean Fontana is an elementary teacher in the Levittown, New York public schools with more than 30 years experience in teaching. Co-founder and first director of the district's teachers' center, she has written numerous articles and presented workshops at state and national conferences.

Allan Glatthorn is Distinguished Research Professor in Education at East Carolina University, in Greenville, North Carolina. An English teacher for more than 20 years, he is the author of 25 professional books, chiefly in the areas of curriculum and supervision. He has also been a high school department chair, principal, and founder and director of two alternative schools.

Kathy Hogan teaches preschool and kindergarten children with disabilities at the Lakeland Elementary School in the Humble, Texas school system. During her 17 years in teaching she has been chosen as Texas Elementary Teacher of the Year (1992-93) and her program has been recognized by the Texas Education Agency (1997-98) as a "promising practice" for inclusion of children with disabilities.

Carol Jago teaches English at Santa Monica High School in Santa Monica, California. She directs the California Reading and Literature Project at the University of California at Los Angeles and edits *California English*, the journal of the California Association of Teachers of English. She has had numerous articles published in national newspapers and educational journals.

James Kelleher, director of curriculum for grades 7-12 in Dover, New Hampshire, holds a doctorate in education from Boston College. Until recently he was a Spanish teacher at Wayland High School, Wayland, Massachusetts.

Patricia McGonegal teaches ninth-and tenth-grade English at Mount Mansfield Union High School in Jericho, Vermont. The director of Vermont's National Writing Project, she is a member of the Bread Loaf Rural Teacher Network and a network leader for the Vermont portfolio assessment system. She has published several articles on professional development and student learning and assessment.

Laura Schiller is a literacy and learning consultant for prekindergarten through grade 12 of the Southfield, Michigan public schools. A National Board Certified teacher and teacher-consultant for the National Writing Project, she is the author of several articles in the field of English language arts and a presenter for the Bureau of Education and Research.

John T. Walsh, a retired U.S. marine, is assistant principal at the Wallace Rose high school in Teachey, North Carolina. Prior to assuming his administrative role, he taught middle school math and science.

Rob Weil, a mathematics teacher at Ponderosa High School in Parker, Colorado, for the past 18 years, is president of the Douglas County, Colorado Federation of Teachers.

5658